Conflict Resolution Education

A Guide to Implementing Programs in
Schools, Youth-Serving Organizations, and
Community and Juvenile Justice Settings

◆

Donna Crawford and Richard Bodine

University Press of the Pacific
Honolulu, Hawaii

Conflict Resolution Education:
A Guide to Implementing Programs in Schools,
Youth-Serving Organizations, and Community and
Juvenile Justice Settings

by
Donna Crawford
Richard Bodine

ISBN: 1-4102-1970-4

Reprinted from the 1996 edition

University Press of the Pacific
Honolulu, Hawaii
http://www.universitypressofthepacific.com

C onflict is a natural, vital part of life. When conflict is understood, it can become an opportunity to learn and create. The challenge for people in conflict is to apply the principles of creative cooperation in their human relationships.

Richard Bodine, Donna Crawford, and Fred Schrumpf
*Creating the Peaceable School: A Comprehensive
Program for Teaching Conflict Resolution*

Foreword

Safe and orderly environments in our Nation's schools are essential to promoting high standards for learning and ensuring that all children have the opportunity to develop to their fullest potential. No teacher should ever fear to walk into a classroom, and no child should ever stay home from school because he or she is afraid. Too often, however, young people face conflicts before, during, and after school. They are subjected to bullying, teasing, and senseless, sometimes fatal, disputes over clothing and other possessions. Many of these conflicts either begin at school, or they are brought into school from the home or the community.

A growing body of evidence suggests that we are not powerless to prevent these destructive behaviors. We can intervene successfully to prevent conflicts from escalating into violent acts by providing young people with the knowledge and skills needed to settle disputes peacefully. Conflict resolution education can help bring about significant reductions in suspensions, disciplinary referrals, academic disruptions, playground fights, and family and sibling disputes. It is important to understand that conflict resolution education is a critical component of comprehensive, community-based efforts to prevent violence and reduce crime.

Conflict Resolution Education: A Guide to Implementing Programs in Schools, Youth-Serving Organizations, and Community and Juvenile Justice Settings was developed for educators, juvenile justice practitioners, and others in youth-serving organizations to heighten awareness of conflict resolution education and its potential to help settle disputes peacefully in a variety of settings. A joint project of the U.S. Department of Justice and the U.S. Department of Education, this *Guide* provides background information on conflict resolution education; an overview of four widely used, promising, and effective approaches; and guidance on how to initiate and implement conflict resolution education programs in various settings.

As adults, we cannot solve young people's problems for them. We can, however, provide them with the knowledge, skills, and encouragement to resolve conflicts in a nonviolent manner, using words instead of fists or weapons. Conflict resolution education includes negotiation, mediation, and consensus decisionmaking, which allow all parties involved to explore peaceful solutions to a conflict. When these problem-solving processes to conflict and strife become a way of life, young people begin to value getting along instead of getting even or getting their way.

We urge you to help make our schools and our communities safer places. We invite you to use this *Guide* as a means of working with your schools, community organizations, and other youth-serving and juvenile justice settings to give our youth the skills, techniques, and tools they need to learn and to resolve disputes in a safe and nonviolent environment.

Janet Reno
Attorney General

Richard W. Riley
Secretary of Education

Acknowledgments

The U.S. Department of Justice (DOJ) and the U.S. Department of Education (ED) recognize the dedication and commitment of Donni LeBoeuf, Senior Program Manager, Office of Juvenile Justice and Delinquency Prevention, Office of Justice Programs, DOJ; and Charlotte Gillespie, Group Leader, Program Service Team, Safe and Drug-Free Schools Program, Office of Elementary and Secondary Education, ED. Their diligence, work, and enthusiasm for this project have helped to bring the vision of this *Guide* to fruition.

We are indebted to Donna Crawford and Richard Bodine of the Illinois Institute for Dispute Resolution who spent countless hours writing and refining the manuscript to convey the variety of approaches within the field of conflict resolution education and the potential of all these approaches for bringing about peaceful resolution of disputes in a number of settings.

We also thank Judith Filner of the National Institute for Dispute Resolution for her work in drafting an initial outline for the manuscript and providing her knowledge of effective and promising programs. In addition, we thank the following members of the Conflict Resolution Education Planning Committee whose ideas and expertise helped bring this project to its completion: Lee Arbetman, Margery Baker, Shay Bilchik, Noël Brennan, Eileen M. Garry, George Henderson, Emily Martin, William Modzeleski, Gail Padgett, John J. Wilson, and Judith Zimmer.

We are grateful to the following individuals for their counsel, guidance, and support throughout this project: Terry Amsler, Ron Ativissimo, Rebecca Atnafou, Vicki Baldwin, Linda Barnes-Robinson, Marcia Choo, Richard Cohen, Irene Cooper-Basch, Jared Curhan, Mary Czajkowski, Robin Delany-Shabazz, Larry Dieringer, Dennis D. Embry, Lucy Friedman, Lynn Glassman, Barbara Greenberg, Mark Greenberg, J. David Hawkins, Shelia Heen, Patti Holman, David Johnson, Ted Johnson, Marianne Klink, Nancy Langan, Linda Lantieri, Linda Lausell, Ray Leal, Raúl Martinez, John Mazzarella, Pamela Moore, Marilyn Moses, Cheryl Niro, Dennis Noonan, Gayle Olson-Raymer, Laura Otey, Kenneth E. Powell, Ellen Raider, Tom Roderick, Laura Parker Roerden, David Roush, Melinda Smith, Ronald Stephens, Susan Stroud, Marcia Sweedler, Annette Townley, Lloyd H. Van Bylevelt, Martin Walsh, and Terry Wheeler. This *Guide* would not have been possible without the steadfast effort and careful review provided by all of these experts and practitioners.

Finally, we wish to express our appreciation to the staff of the Juvenile Justice Resource Center, especially Laurie Shah and Janet McNaughton, who gathered information, edited the manuscript, and prepared the document for publication. Additionally, the Juvenile Justice Clearinghouse, under the guidance of Catherine Doyle, deserves our thanks for their work in bringing the final manuscript through the publication process.

Table of Contents

List of Figures

List of Tables

Prologue

"Grandmother," she said, "what big arms you have!"
"The better to hug you with, my dear."

"Grandmother, what big legs you have!"
"The better to run with, my child."

"Grandmother, what big eyes you have!"
"The better to see, my child."

"Grandmother, what big teeth you have!"
"They're to eat you with!" And at these words, the wicked wolf pounced on
Little Red Ridinghood and ate her up.

—"Little Red Ridinghood"[1]

WOLF: Now wait a minute, Red. I know your granny. I thought we should teach you a lesson for prancing on my pine trees in that get-up and for picking my flowers. I let you go on your way in the woods but I ran ahead to your granny's cottage.

When I saw Granny, I explained what happened, and she agreed that you needed to learn a lesson. Granny hid under the bed, and I dressed up in her nightgown.

When you came into the bedroom, you saw me in the bed and said something nasty about my big ears. I've been told my ears are big before, so I tried to make the best of it by saying big ears help me hear you better.

Then you made an insulting crack about my bulging eyes. This one was really hard to blow off, because you sounded so nasty. Still, I make it a policy to turn the other cheek, so I told you my big eyes help me see you better.

Your next insult about my big teeth really got to me. You see, I'm quite sensitive about my teeth. I know that when you made fun of my teeth I should have had better control, but I leaped from the bed and growled that my teeth would help me to eat you.

But, come on, Red! Let's face it. Everyone knows no Wolf could ever eat a girl, but you started screaming and running around the house. I tried to catch you to calm you down.

All of a sudden the door came crashing open, and a big woodsman stood there with his ax. I knew I was in trouble . . . there was an open window behind me, so out I went.

I've been hiding ever since. There are terrible rumors going around the forest about me. Red, you called me the Big Bad Wolf. I'd like to say I've gotten over feeling bad, but the truth is I haven't lived happily ever after.

I don't understand why Granny never told you and the others my side of the story. I'm upset about the rumors and have been afraid to show my face in the forest. Why have you and Granny let the situation go on for this long? It just isn't fair. I'm miserable and lonely.

RED: You think that I have started unfair rumors about you, and you are miserable and lonely and don't understand why Granny didn't tell your side of the story.

Well, Granny has been sick—and she's been very tired lately. When I asked her how she came to be under the bed, she said she couldn't remember a thing that had happened. Come to think of it, she didn't seem too upset . . . just confused.

—"The Story of Little Red Riding Hood and the Wolf,
Retold Through Negotiation"[2]

Fairytales and folktales are read to children to entertain them, but these stories also communicate common ideas and modes of thinking about relationships, morals, values, and how to get along in the world. Fairytales present children with a model of how to think and act. In the original story of Little Red Riding Hood, one of the morals is to beware of strangers. The two sides in this fairytale are sharply drawn—one good, one bad; one innocent, one cunning; one right, one wrong. If the retelling of the tale seems odd, it is because it challenges the stereotype of the "Big Bad Wolf" and asks us to consider his side of the story.

The tenets of conflict resolution present a new model of interacting with and thinking about other people—one that challenges us to go beyond stereotypes, to consider the other's point of view, and to reach mutually satisfactory agreements in which all parties win. "The Story of Little Red Riding Hood and the Wolf, Retold Through Negotiation," which is reprinted in its entirety in appendix I, is an illustration of one of the problem-solving processes of conflict resolution. If we can succeed in teaching our youth this framework for resolving their disputes, the results for them and for our society could be profound.

Notes

1. Bierhorst, J. (translator). 1981. *The Glass Slipper: Charles Perrault's Tales of Times Past.* New York: Four Winds Press.

2. Bodine, R., D. Crawford, and F. Schrumpf. 1994. *Creating the Peaceable School: A Comprehensive Program for Teaching Conflict Resolution.* Champaign, IL: Research Press, Inc.

Introduction

This *Guide* was developed through a collaboration of the Departments of Justice and Education to advance the development of conflict resolution education programs in schools, youth-serving organizations, and community and juvenile justice settings. It is designed to be a reference tool that offers both basic information and the experience of experts in the field of conflict resolution to assist educators and other youth-serving professionals in building effective conflict resolution education programs. The *Guide* is based on a shared vision that youth of all ages can learn to deal constructively with conflict and live in civil association with one another. Its goal is to build the capacity of educators in a variety of youth-serving settings to understand and act on the knowledge that conflict resolution skills are essential to successful relationships in all facets of our lives.

Purposes of Conflict Resolution Education

To fulfill their mission of educating youth and preparing them to function effectively in adult society, American schools* must first be safe places. Our schools are challenged to provide an environment in which:

◆ Each learner can feel physically and psychologically free from threats and danger and can find opportunities to work and learn with others for the mutual achievement of all.

◆ The diversity of the school's population is respected and celebrated.

---

*Throughout this *Guide*, the term "school" is intended to encompass youth-serving organizations and programs in community and juvenile justice settings in addition to traditional schools.

We have a juvenile justice system that in many states is bankrupt and is starting too late. You cannot start with a 16- or 17-year-old who has dropped out of school and who was the drug dealer's gofer when he was 13. You've got to start earlier. . . . We can do tremendous amounts of good through conflict resolution programs in our public schools.

Attorney General Janet Reno[1]

Conflict resolution programs can help schools promote both the individual behavioral change necessary for responsible citizenship and the systemic change necessary for a safe learning environment.

Responsible Citizenship

The ability to resolve disputes effectively and nonviolently is central to the peaceful expression of human rights. Conflict resolution can be viewed as a responsibility of law-abiding members of our society. Responsible citizens in a democracy express their concerns peacefully and seek resolutions to problems that take into account common interests and recognize the human dignity of all involved.

Schools can be places where children learn to live in civil association with one another and prepare to assume their future roles as parents, as community members and leaders, and as productive members of the workforce. Conflict resolution skills are essential to public life in schools, communities, and workplaces. These skills encompass more than a set of complex problem-solving processes. The ability to resolve larger issues depends, at least to some extent, on how people deal with each other daily. Building effective relationships among citizens is important not just for reaching agreements, but for shaping how people choose to disagree.[2]

Education can be turned into a force for reducing intergroup conflict. It can emphasize common characteristics and goals and can broaden our understanding of diverse cultures, even in circumstances of conflict. The question is whether human beings can develop a constructive orientation toward those outside their group while maintaining the values of group allegiance and identity. It seems reasonable to believe that, in spite of very bad habits from the past and very bad models in the present, we can indeed learn new habits of mind: "It is not too late for a paradigm shift in our outlook toward human conflict. Perhaps it is something like learning that the earth is not flat. Such a shift in child development and education . . . might at long last make it possible for human groups to learn to live together in peace and mutual benefit."[3]

Many conflicts in schools arise out of differences. Cultural conflicts are based on differences in national origin or ethnicity. Social conflicts are based on differences in gender, sexual orientation, class, and physical and mental abilities. Personal and institutional reactions to differences often take the form of prejudice, discrimination, harassment, and even hate crimes. These conflicts are complex because they are rooted not only in prejudice and discrimination related to cultural and social differences but also in the resulting structures and relationships of inequality and privilege. Conflict resolution education programs provide a framework for addressing these problems. The programs promote respect and acceptance through new ways of communicating and understanding.

Conflict resolution education offers schools strategies for responding affirmatively to the following questions:[4]

♦ Do members of school communities possess the skills and knowledge to create an environment in which diversity thrives and in which tolerance of differences is encouraged?

♦ Do members share a cultivated willingness to accept the inevitable conflict that arises from differing values and cultures within the school community?

♦ Are the participants in the school community convinced that conflict is an opportunity for growth, self-awareness, and development of understanding and respect for others?

♦ Do the participants in the school community articulate a shared vision that conflicts are inevitable and that they enrich and strengthen school communities?

Young people must be challenged to believe and to act on the understanding that a nonviolent, multicultural society is a desirable, realistic goal.[5]

> The best school-based violence prevention programs seek to do more than reach the individual child. They instead try to change the total school environment, to create a safe community that lives by a credo of nonviolence.
>
> *William DeJong, Harvard School of Public Health*[6]

Violence Prevention and Safe Schools

Strategies that empower students to deal constructively with interpersonal conflicts, cultural differences, and the violence embedded in American culture need to be grounded in day-to-day experience. The fundamental challenge is to engage young people in learning the skills and processes that will enable them to manage and resolve conflict constructively. When youth experience success with negotiation, mediation, or consensus decisionmaking in school or other youth-serving settings, they are more likely to use these conflict resolution processes elsewhere in their lives.

Schools alone cannot change a violent society; however, they can:

♦ Teach alternatives to violence.

- Teach students to act responsibly in social settings.

- Teach students to understand and accept the consequences of their behavior.

Conflict resolution education provides youth with the knowledge, abilities, and processes needed to choose alternatives to self-destructive, violent behavior when confronted with interpersonal and intergroup conflict. The expectation is that when youth learn constructive ways to address what leads to violence, the incidence and intensity of that conflict will diminish.

Systemic Change

A conflict resolution program provides an effective alternative to a traditional discipline program. Youth who grow up in circumstances in which they are socialized to violence, physical abuse, or even death will not be brought readily into submission by such punishments as lowered grades, time out, detention, suspension, or even expulsion. Alternatives that lead to long-term changes in attitudes and behavior are needed. Conflict resolution programs are an important part of those alternatives because they invite participation and expect those who choose to participate to plan more effective behavior and then to behave accordingly.[7]

To realize maximum results from conflict resolution education programs, schools need to examine their systems and, if necessary, reform them to create a context that facilitates the development and support of the program. Systemic change calls for cooperation to be the normative expectation, both behaviorally and academically, and for adults to interact noncoercively with youth. The goal of making school a safe haven in which youth can gain respite from violence in order to think and learn is a good one. However, it cannot be realized apart from creating an antiviolent vision shared by everyone in the building.[8]

Conflict resolution, when implemented not only as a curriculum to be taught but as a lifestyle to be lived by both adults and youth, fosters continuous academic and social growth. Implementation of a conflict resolution program can help schools create their governance structures, develop policies, identify goals, make curriculum decisions, and plan for assessment of learning. Faculty and students work and learn together while supporting one another. When conflict resolution is practiced by all, respect, caring, tolerance, and community building become "the way we do things around here."[9]

> The significant problems we face cannot be solved at the same level of thinking we were at when we created them.
>
> *Albert Einstein*

Rationale for Establishing Conflict Resolution Programs

There are compelling, valid reasons for every school to implement a program to teach youth conflict resolution:[10]

- The problem-solving processes of conflict resolution (negotiation, mediation, and consensus decisionmaking) can improve the school climate.

- Conflict resolution strategies can reduce violence, vandalism, chronic school absence, and suspension.

- Conflict resolution training helps students and teachers deepen their understanding of themselves and others and develops important life skills.

- Training in negotiation, mediation, and consensus decisionmaking encourages a high level of citizenship activity.

- Shifting the responsibility for solving nonviolent conflicts to students frees adults to concentrate more on teaching and less on discipline.

- Behavior management systems that are more effective than detention, suspension, or expulsion are needed to deal with conflict in the school setting.

- Conflict resolution training increases skills in listening, critical thinking, and problem solving — skills basic to all learning.

- Conflict resolution education emphasizes seeing other points of view and resolving differences peacefully — skills that assist one to live in a multicultural world.

- Negotiation and mediation are problem-solving tools that are well suited to the problems that young people face, and those trained in these approaches often use them to solve problems for which they would not seek adult help.

How the *Guide* Is Organized

This *Guide* is designed to provide sufficient information and tools to initiate the development of comprehensive youth-centered conflict resolution programs. It provides a framework for making informed decisions to implement conflict resolution education programs and select resources to support program development.

Chapter 1, "Understanding Conflict Resolution," defines conflict as a natural condition and examines the origins of conflict, responses to conflict, and the outcomes of those responses. It presents the essential principles, foundation abilities, and problem-solving processes of conflict resolution; discusses the elements of a successful conflict resolution program; and introduces four approaches to implementing conflict resolution education.

Each of the next four chapters discusses one of these four approaches and presents examples of programs that use the approach. Chapter 2, "Process Curriculum Approach," describes an approach to conflict resolution education characterized by devoting a specific time to teaching the foundation abilities, principles, and one or more of the problem-solving processes of conflict resolution in a separate course or distinct curriculum. Chapter 3, "Mediation Program Approach," describes an approach in which selected individuals who have been trained in the principles and foundation abilities of conflict resolution and in the mediation process provide neutral,

third-party facilitation to help those in conflict to reach resolution. Chapter 4, "Peaceable Classroom Approach," presents an approach that incorporates conflict resolution education into the core subject areas of the curriculum and into classroom management strategies. Chapter 5, "Peaceable School Approach," presents a comprehensive whole-school methodology that builds on the peaceable classroom approach, using conflict resolution as a system of operation for managing the school as well as the classroom.

The next two chapters address conflict resolution education in settings other than traditional schools. Chapter 6, "Juvenile Justice and Alternative Education Initiatives," discusses conflict resolution education in juvenile justice facilities and alternative schools. Chapter 7, "Parent and Community Initiatives," examines linkages between conflict resolution education programs in schools and the greater community, including programs for parents and youth.

The final three chapters address more overarching topics. Chapter 8, "Conflict Resolution Research and Evaluation," reviews research findings on conflict resolution education programs in schools and considers the value of conflict resolution education in the light of developmental research on resilience and risk factors. Chapter 9, "Developmentally Appropriate Practice," presents a developmental sequence of behavioral expectations intended to provide guideposts for developing and assessing proficiency in conflict resolution from kindergarten through high school. Chapter 10, "Establishing Conflict Resolution Education Programs," discusses the process of developing, implementing, and sustaining a conflict resolution program.

The appendices to the *Guide* offer a variety of resources for those establishing conflict resolution education programs. Appendix A, "Contact Information," lists addresses and telephone numbers of organizations that provide national leadership in the field of conflict resolution education. Appendix B, "Conflict Resolution Curriculum Resources," is an annotated compilation of conflict resolution curriculums and texts. Appendix C, "Conflict Resolution Reading List," presents the titles of recommended articles and books on conflict resolution. Every program, resource, or text mentioned in the *Guide* is referenced either in one of these three appendices or in a chapter endnote. A glossary of conflict resolution terminology is given in appendix D. Appendices E through G contain sample forms, including forms for assessing staff and programs/curriculums. Appendix H presents the components essential to a strategic plan for implementing a conflict resolution program. The complete text of the Little Red Riding Hood story retold through negotiation, excerpted in the prologue, is found in appendix I.

Notes

1. Goldberg, S.B., and H.J. Reske. 1993. "Talking with Attorney General Janet Reno." *American Bar Association Journal* 79:46.

2. Amsler, T. 1994 (March). "Educating for Citizenship: Reframing Conflict Resolution Work in K–12 Schools." Paper presented at the Coulson Festshrift Meeting, Aspen Institute, Wye Conference Center, Queenstown, Maryland, March 13–14, 1994.

3. Hamburg, D. 1994. *Education for Conflict Resolution*. Report of the President of the Carnegie Corporation of New York, p. 15.

4. Adapted from Townley, A. "Introduction: Conflict Resolution, Diversity and Social Justice." *Education and Urban Society* 27(1), pp. 5–10, copyright © 1994 by Corwin Press. Reprinted by permission of Corwin Press, Inc.

5. Moore, P., and D. Batiste. 1994 (Spring). "Preventing Youth Violence: Prejudice Elimination and Conflict Resolution Programs." *Forum*, no. 25, p. 18.

6. DeJong, W. 1994 (Spring). "School-Based Violence Prevention: From the Peaceable School to the Peaceable Neighborhood." *Forum*, no. 25, p. 8.

7. Bodine, R., and D. Crawford. In press. *Developing Emotional Intelligence Through Classroom Management: Creating Responsible Learners in Our Schools and Effective Citizens for Our World*. Champaign, IL: Research Press, Inc.

8. Haberman, M., and V. Schreiber Dill. 1995. "Commitment to Violence Among Teenagers in Poverty." *Kappa Delta Pi Record* 31(4):149.

9. Adler, A. 1995. "Implementing District-Wide Programs: If I Knew Then What I Know Now." *The Fourth R* 57:5.

10. Adapted from Davis, A., and K. Porter. 1985 (Spring). "Dispute Resolution: The Fourth R." *Journal of Dispute Resolution*, 1985:121–139. Reprinted with permission of the authors and of the Center for the Study of Dispute Resolution, University of Missouri-Columbia School of Law.

Chapter 1: Understanding Conflict Resolution

Conflict arises from a discord of needs, drives, wishes, and/or demands. Conflict in and of itself is not positive or negative. Rather, it is the response to conflict that transforms it into either a competitive, destructive experience or a constructive challenge offering the opportunity for growth. Since conflict is an inevitable part of life, learning how to respond to it constructively is essential. Constructive conflict resolution begins with developing an understanding of conflict and the principles of conflict resolution (see figure 1).

Origins of Conflict

Almost every conflict involves an attempt by the disputants to meet basic needs that, if not satisfied, cause the conflict to persist, even when an agreement is reached about the subject of the dispute.[1]

Basic Psychological Needs

All individuals are motivated by needs. Dr. William Glasser identifies four basic psychological needs that motivate behavior:[2]

♦ **Belonging:** Fulfilled by loving, sharing, and cooperating with others.

♦ **Power:** Fulfilled by achieving, accomplishing, and being recognized and respected.

♦ **Freedom:** Fulfilled by making choices.

♦ **Fun:** Fulfilled by laughing and playing.

Conflicts may occur, for example, when two individuals in a relationship have different ideas about how to belong or because one is more concerned with building the relationship and the other with maintaining a sense

Learning can take place only when schools are safe, disciplined, and drug free. Schools in all types of communities—urban, rural, and suburban—are taking steps to be free of violent and disruptive behavior. Incorporating conflict resolution education into the curriculum can be an important step in ensuring a safe and healthy learning environment.

Secretary of Education Richard W. Riley

of freedom. When conflict arises, individuals have essentially two choices: to continue the conflict or to problem-solve. The problem-solving strategies of conflict resolution address needs and create opportunities for those needs to be satisfied. When individuals choose to continue the conflict, no one's basic needs are fulfilled. Basic psychological needs are at the root of almost all conflict.

Limited Resources

Conflicts may arise over limited resources. Conflict resolution principles suggest that when limited resources are at issue, individuals' best interests lie in cooperating, not competing. In cooperating, disputants share in the process of problem solving, recognize each other's interests, and create choices. This process usually provides satisfaction because the psychological needs of belonging and power, and perhaps even of freedom and fun, are addressed in the fair allocation of limited resources.

Conflicts over limited resources may not be resolved if basic needs are not addressed along with the resource issue. The resource issue by itself may not

Figure 1: Understanding Conflict

Origins of Conflict		
Limited Resources	**Unmet Basic Needs**	**Different Values**
Time	Belonging	Beliefs
Money	Power	Priorities
Property	Freedom	Principles
	Fun	

C o n f l i c t

Responses to Conflict		
Soft	**Hard**	**Principled**
Withdrawing	Threatening	Listening
Ignoring	Pushing	Understanding
Denying	Hitting	Respecting
Giving in	Yelling	Resolving

Outcomes to Conflict		
Soft	**Hard**	**Principled**
Lose-Lose	Lose-Lose	Win-Win
Lose-Win	Win-Lose	

Source: Bodine, R., D. Crawford, and F. Schrumpf. 1994. *Creating the Peaceable School: A Comprehensive Program for Teaching Conflict Resolution.* Champaign, IL: Research Press, Inc., p. 92. Reprinted with permission of the authors and Research Press.

define the problem. When solutions deal only with the limited resource that appears to be the source of the conflict without addressing other underlying interests, conflict between the parties will likely occur again.

Different Values

Conflicts involving different values (beliefs, priorities, principles) tend to be more difficult to resolve. When an individual holds a value, he or she has an enduring belief that a specific action or quality is preferable to another action or quality. Many times disputants think in terms of "right/wrong" or "good/bad" when values are in opposition. Even conflicts over differing goals can be viewed as value conflicts. The source of a goal conflict relates either to the goal's relative importance for each disputant or to the fact that the disputants value different goals.

Resolving a values conflict does not mean the disputants must change or agree on their values. Often a mutual acknowledgment that each person views the situation differently is the first step toward resolution. If the disputants can learn not to reject each other because of differences in beliefs, they will be better able to deal with the problem on its own merits. One of the fundamental principles of conflict resolution is to address separately the relationship issues and the substantive issues involved in the conflict. To resolve values conflicts, the disputants must look for interests that underlie the conflicting values. Again, psychological needs are enmeshed in values conflicts, and those needs likely frame the interests of each disputant.

Values disputes may be rooted in issues of social diversity (differences in cultural, social, and physical/mental attributes), which are often expressed as different beliefs, convictions, and/or principles. Issues of social diversity also often involve prejudice. Although complex, these conflicts can be resolved by increased awareness, understanding, and respect. When a conflict is rooted in prejudice or bias against another, ignorance, fear, and misunderstanding often guide behavior toward that person.

Responses to Conflict

Responses to conflict can be categorized into three basic groups: *soft, hard,* and *principled* responses.[3] In both soft and hard responses, disputants take positions or stands relative to the problem. They negotiate these positions by trying either to avoid or to win a contest of wills. Soft and hard negotiations either bring about one-sided losses or demand one-sided gains. In principled responses, disputants use conflict resolution strategies to produce lasting "wise agreements" that address the legitimate interests of both parties, resolve conflicting interests fairly, and take into account how others will be affected by the agreement.

Soft responses such as avoidance, accommodation, and compromise usually occur between individuals who are friends or who want to be pleasant to each other because they will continue to have contact in the future. Individuals may attempt to avoid conflict altogether by withdrawing from the situation, ignoring it, or denying that the conflict even matters. Accommodation involves one disputant giving in to the position of the other without seeking to serve his or her interests. Disputants who compromise agree to something that does not really address the interests of either one in order to end the dispute. Soft responses typically result in feelings of disillusionment, self-doubt, fear, and anxiety about the future.

Hard responses to conflict usually occur between individuals who are adversaries and whose goal is victory. Hard responses to a conflict are characterized by confrontations that involve force, threats, aggression, and anger. Hard negotiators demand concessions as a condition of the relationship and insist on their position. They often search for a single answer to the problem—namely, the one the other side will give in to. Hard negotiators frequently apply pressure, trying to win a contest of wills. They use bribery and punishments such as withholding money, favors, and affection. Hard responses are detrimental to cooperation and relationships and often result in hostility, physical damage, and violence.

Principled responses occur between individuals who view themselves as problem solvers and whose goal is a wise outcome reached efficiently and amicably. Principled negotiators understand that communication is fundamental to cooperative interaction, and they understand what it means to participate in developing a common understanding. Principled negotiators are skilled, active, empathic listeners. They attempt to see the problem from different perspectives. Principled responses to conflict create the opportunity for the needs of both disputants to be met through an agreement that addresses the interests of both. Principled responses to conflict preserve relationships.

Outcomes of Soft, Hard, and Principled Responses

The three types of responses to conflict produce different outcomes. *Soft* responses typically result in two types of outcomes. In situations in which individuals give in on their positions for the sake of the relationship, with the result that no one's interests are met, lose-lose outcomes result. In situations in which one side accommodates the other, lose-win outcomes occur. Individuals who avoid conflict by accommodating others lose, in the sense that their basic needs are not acknowledged or met. Often, individuals who avoid conflict see themselves as victims, and their relations with others suffer.

Hard responses also typically result in two types of outcomes. Win-lose outcomes occur when the more aggressive party wins and the adversary loses. Hard responses to conflict often lead to a situation in which the desire to punish or get even provokes adversaries to take vindictive actions that harm themselves as well as their opponents. This results in a lose-lose outcome. Stressful situations follow when these adversaries are required to continue to interact in some manner.

Principled responses to conflict typically lead to a win-win outcome. Using a problem-solving process based on principled negotiation theory, individuals in conflict come to consensus on a joint resolution without locking into positions or destroying relationships. The interests and needs of each party in the dispute are met.

Problem-Solving Processes

The structured problem-solving processes of conflict resolution are *negotiation, mediation,* and *consensus decisionmaking.*[4] All problem-solving processes in conflict resolution are based on integrated negotiation theory. In conflict resolution literature and practice, the terms "negotiation" and "mediation" are often used interchangeably. In this *Guide*, the three structured problem-solving processes are defined as follows:

♦ **Negotiation** is a problem-solving process in which either the two parties in the dispute or their representatives meet face to face to work together unassisted to resolve the dispute between the parties.

♦ **Mediation** is a problem-solving process in which the two parties in the dispute or their representatives meet face to face to work together to resolve the dispute assisted by a neutral third party called the "mediator."

♦ **Consensus decisionmaking** is a group problem-solving process in which all of the parties in the dispute or representatives of each party collaborate to resolve the dispute by crafting a plan of action that all parties can and will support. This process may or may not be facilitated by a neutral party.

Principles of Conflict Resolution

Effective implementation of the conflict resolution processes of negotiation, mediation, or consensus decisionmaking requires an understanding of the following four essential principles:

♦ **Separate people from the problem.** Every problem involves both substantive issues and relationship issues. By separating these issues, individuals come to see themselves as working side by side, attacking the problem, not each other. Fisher and colleagues state, "Where perceptions are inaccurate, you can look for ways to educate. If emotions run high, you can find ways for each person involved to let off steam. Where misunderstanding exists, you can work to improve communication."[5]

♦ **Focus on interests, not positions.** Understanding the difference between positions and interests is crucial to problem solving. Interests, not positions, define the problem. Positions are something that individuals decide they want; interests are the underlying motivations behind the positions they take. Fisher and colleagues note that "compromising between positions is not likely to produce an agreement which will effectively take care of the human needs that led individuals to adopt those positions."[6] Where such interests are not identified, temporary agreements may be reached, but typically do not last because the real interests have not been addressed.

♦ **Invent options for mutual gain.** Disputants focus on identifying options for resolving the conflict without the pressure of reaching a decision. A brainstorming process is used to invent a wide range of options that advance shared interests and creatively reconcile differing interests. The key ground rule to brainstorming is to postpone criticism and evaluation of the ideas being generated.

To broaden their options, those in a dispute think about the problem in different ways and build upon the ideas presented.

♦ **Use objective criteria.** Using objective criteria ensures that the agreement reflects some fair standard instead of the arbitrary will of either side. Using objective criteria means that neither party needs to give in to the other; rather, they can defer to a fair solution. Objective criteria are determined by disputants based on fair standards and fair procedures.[7]

Foundation Abilities for Conflict Resolution

Effective implementation of the problem-solving processes of conflict resolution requires various attitudes, understandings, and skills for dealing with a problem or dispute. Conflict resolution occurs when individuals change from being adversaries in a face-to-face confrontation to being partners in a side-by-side search for a fair agreement that is advantageous to both. Training in the six foundation abilities of conflict resolution helps to promote the effective use of the four principles of conflict resolution. The six foundation abilities are as follows:

♦ **Orientation abilities** encompass values, beliefs, attitudes, and propensities that are compatible with effective conflict resolution. Orientation abilities include:

◇ Nonviolence.

◇ Compassion and empathy.

◇ Fairness.

◇ Trust.

◇ Justice.

◇ Tolerance.

◇ Self-respect.

◇ Respect for others.

◇ Celebration of diversity.

◇ Appreciation for controversy.

♦ **Perception abilities** encompass the understanding that conflict lies not in objective reality, but in how individuals perceive that reality. Perception abilities include:

◇ Empathizing in order to see the situation as the other side sees it.

◇ Self-evaluating to recognize personal fears.

◇ Suspending judgment and blame to facilitate a free exchange of views.

♦ **Emotion abilities** encompass behaviors to manage anger, frustration, fear, and other emotions effectively. Emotion abilities include:

◇ Learning language for communicating emotions effectively.

◇ Expressing emotions in nonaggressive, noninflammatory ways.

◇ Exercising self-control in order not to react to the emotional outbursts of others.

♦ **Communication abilities** encompass behaviors of listening and speaking that allow for the effective exchange of facts and feelings. Communication abilities include:

◇ Listening to understand by using active listening behaviors.

◇ Speaking to be understood.

◇ Reframing emotionally charged statements into neutral, less emotional terms.

♦ **Creative thinking abilities** encompass behaviors that enable individuals to be innovative in defining problems and making decisions. Creative thinking abilities include:

◇ Contemplating the problem from a variety of perspectives.

◇ Approaching the problem-solving task as a mutual pursuit of possibilities.

◇ Brainstorming to create, elaborate, and enhance a variety of options.

- **Critical thinking abilities** encompass the behaviors of analyzing, hypothesizing, predicting, strategizing, comparing/contrasting, and evaluating. Critical thinking abilities include:

  ◇ Recognizing existing criteria and making them explicit.

  ◇ Establishing objective criteria.

  ◇ Applying criteria as the basis for choosing options.

  ◇ Planning future behaviors.

Although these foundation abilities are necessary to the successful implementation of the problem-solving processes of conflict resolution, programs that teach only these skills are not genuine conflict resolution programs.

Steps in the Problem-Solving Process

Genuine conflict resolution programs require two major components: the principles of conflict resolution (separate the people from the problem; focus on interests, not positions; invent options for mutual gain; and use objective criteria as the basis for decision-making) and a problem-solving process (negotiation, mediation, or consensus decisionmaking). The conflict resolution processes are characterized by a series of steps that enable the disputants to identify their own needs and interests and to work cooperatively to find solutions to meet those needs and interests. Each process gives support and direction to the cooperative effort, assisting the parties to stay focused on the problem rather than on each other and to find a mutually acceptable resolution. In addition, genuine conflict resolution education programs include extensive training and practice using the principles and problem-solving processes of conflict resolution.

The six steps in each problem-solving process are:

- Set the stage.

- Gather perspectives.

- Identify interests.

- Create options.

- Evaluate options.

- Generate agreement.

Approaches to Conflict Resolution Education

There are four basic approaches to conflict resolution education in operation across the country:

- **Process Curriculum:** An approach to conflict resolution education characterized by devoting a specific time to teaching the foundation abilities, principles, and one or more of the problem-solving processes of conflict resolution as a separate course, distinct curriculum, or daily lesson plan.

- **Mediation Program:** A conflict resolution education program in which selected individuals (adults and/or students) are trained in the principles and foundation abilities of conflict resolution and in the mediation process in order to provide neutral third-party facilitation to assist those in conflict to reach a resolution.

- **Peaceable Classroom:** A whole-classroom methodology that includes teaching students the foundation abilities, principles, and one or more of the three problem-solving processes of conflict resolution. Conflict resolution education is incorporated into the core subjects of the curriculum and into classroom management strategies. Peaceable classrooms are the building blocks of the peaceable school.

- **Peaceable School:** A comprehensive whole-school methodology that builds on the peaceable classroom approach by using conflict resolution as a system of operation for managing the school as well as the classroom. Conflict resolution principles and processes are learned and utilized by every member of the school community—librarians, teachers, counselors, students, principals, and parents.

The lines dividing these four approaches are sometimes difficult to draw in practice, but the categories can be useful in describing the focus of each approach. The strength of each approach lies in its application of the conflict resolution principles and problem-solving processes. Some of the best programs have evolved in schools where the principles and problem-solving processes of conflict resolution allowed for gradual expansion from one approach to another.

Each of these approaches to conflict resolution education is described in detail in the next four chapters. Operational examples of each approach are included to illustrate the variety of options for program implementation. These representative programs were selected through a nomination process by national leaders in the field of conflict resolution education. Programs were chosen for their advancement of knowledge, teaching, and comprehensive support for the peaceful resolution of disputes among all people, regardless of age, race, ethnic background, or socioeconomic status. Their selection does not constitute an endorsement by either the Department of Justice or the Department of Education. Readers are encouraged to inform themselves about the range of programs available and the purposes of these programs.

Notes

1. The discussion in this section is adapted, with the permission of the authors and of Research Press, Inc., from Bodine, R., D. Crawford, and F. Schrumpf. 1994. *Creating the Peaceable School: A Comprehensive Program for Teaching Conflict Resolution*. Champaign, IL: Research Press, Inc., pp. 52–53.

2. Glasser, W. 1984. *Control Theory*. New York, NY: Harper & Row.

3. The discussion in this section is adapted, with the permission of the authors and of Research Press, Inc., from Bodine et al., *Creating the Peaceable School*, p. 54.

4. The discussion in this section is adapted, with the permission of the authors and of Research Press, Inc., from Bodine et al., *Creating the Peaceable School*, pp. 56–57.

5. Fisher, R., W. Ury, and B. Patton. 1991. *Getting To Yes: Negotiating Agreement Without Giving In*. New York, NY: Penguin Books, p. 21.

6. Ibid., p. 11.

7. Ibid., p. 15.

Chapter 2: Process Curriculum Approach

Process Curriculum: An approach to conflict resolution education characterized by devoting a specific time to teaching the foundation abilities, principles, and one or more of the problem-solving processes of conflict resolution as a separate course, distinct curriculum, or daily lesson plan.

Teachers who use the process curriculum approach teach conflict resolution through a time-limited course, daily lessons over the length of a semester, or a series of workshops, perhaps conducted during the homeroom advisory period in middle and high schools. The daily lesson method is most often part of elementary school offerings. Although the process curriculum could be integrated into the existing curriculum, teachers usually present it separately. The lessons, which cover the principles and problem-solving processes of conflict resolution, are unified in scope and sequence, taking place through structured activities such as simulations, role-plays, group discussions, and cooperative learning activities. This chapter describes three examples of the process curriculum approach.

The Program for Young Negotiators

The Program for Young Negotiators (PYN), a process curriculum program developed by Jared Curhan, aims to teach individuals how to achieve their goals without violence.[1] Participating students, teachers, and administrators are taught a means of goal achievement and dispute resolution that has at its heart the practice of principled negotiation. This type of negotiation challenges the notion that disputes are resolved only when one side wins at the other's expense, and it helps students envision

> Have you not learned great lessons from those who braced themselves against you, and disputed the passage with you?
>
> *Walt Whitman*

scenarios and generate options in which *both* sides are satisfied with the outcome and both are able to achieve their goals. The foundation abilities of perception and thinking that are taught in negotiation courses help students learn that, to satisfy their own interests, they must empathize with the interests of others.

PYN consists of four components:

♦ Teacher training and community involvement.

♦ Negotiation curriculums.

♦ Followup opportunities.

♦ Ongoing curriculum development and innovation.

Teacher Training and Community Involvement

The program first trains schoolteachers and administrators to negotiate their own issues. During a training seminar, participants learn negotiation from professionals such as negotiation professors and practicing negotiators. After teachers begin teaching negotiation concepts to their students, they continue to attend regular curriculum implementation meetings and are provided with ongoing technical support.

Each teacher may request up to three community volunteers, who are recruited by the program, to help implement his or her first negotiation course. A diverse corps of volunteer teaching assistants includes professional negotiators, graduate students, parents, and community leaders. Volunteer teaching assistants make a commitment to attend training seminars and learn and teach negotiation techniques with their partner teachers.

Negotiation Curriculum

The PYN curriculum is based on the seven basic elements of negotiation that have been developed by the Harvard Negotiation Project (figure 2). The curriculum presents negotiation skills not simply as an alternative to violence, but as a necessary condition for a successful and meaningful life. As in successful adult negotiation courses, the curriculum relies heavily on experiential learning. The courses begin with cases that highlight basic principles, but as the curriculum unfolds, examples are increasingly drawn from the lives of teenagers. The students actively participate in games and role-play exercises. Through mock negotiations, they experience empowerment first hand as they learn to collaborate, communicate carefully, and think in a win-win manner.

> Now, because of PYN, I don't have to argue with my brother—we can sit down and talk.
>
> *Seventh grader,*
> *Charlestown, Massachusetts*

Followup Opportunities

When teachers complete the basic curriculum in the classroom, they are presented with a number of followup opportunities. Each teacher receives a list of the following options:

◆ Training a new group of students with the same curriculum.

◆ Integrating the negotiation concepts into a subject area.

> The results of the program were dramatic. The class we targeted for the PYN course had a history of being the most disruptive in the seventh grade. Those same students have internalized the skills they learned in PYN, resulting in a marked change in behavior. Students think before they speak, dialog using negotiation, and offer negotiation to other students as an acceptable option for solving conflicts.
>
> *Principal, Roxbury, Massachusetts*

◆ Arranging negotiation workshops for parents and community members.

◆ Developing a Young Negotiators Club.

◆ Training student council members.

◆ Holding weekly or monthly negotiation periods in which students help each other with their personal conflicts.

◆ Organizing student focus groups to develop new teaching cases.

Ongoing Curriculum Development and Innovation

Throughout each semester, PYN collects feedback from teachers and other training participants. New cases are developed for the curriculum, and existing ones are modified as part of the ongoing curriculum development and revision process. Each year, teachers receive revisions or newly submitted cases developed during the previous year. For example, one teacher developed a negotiation case in his history class to present the issue of Mayan farmers and landholding; he submitted this case to PYN for history teachers to use.

Violence prevention is an important benefit of PYN courses, but negotiation theory can also be applied in circumstances where violence is not imminent. From inner-city neighborhoods to small country towns, negotiation skills are universally applicable

Figure 2: Seven Elements of Negotiation

Harvard Negotiation Project	Program for Young Negotiators
◆ **Communicate** unconditionally both ways.	◆ Understand their **perceptions** and communicate your own.
◆ Build a **relationship** in which you work side by side.	◆ Be **trustworthy** all the time and collaborate.
◆ Clarify everyone's underlying **interests**.	◆ Explore their underlying **interests**, as well as your own.
◆ Without commitment, generate **options** to meet the interests.	◆ **Brainstorm** options without criticizing each other.
◆ Find external standards of **legitimacy** by which to evaluate and improve options.	◆ Identify **fair reasons** for choosing options.
◆ Think about the walk-away **alternatives** if no agreement is reached.	◆ Know your **backup plan**.
◆ Carefully draft terms that are better than the best alternatives. Then make **commitments**.	◆ **Package** options based on both of your interests.

Source: Adapted with permission from materials of the Harvard Negotiation Project, Harvard Law School, Cambridge, Massachusetts, and of the Program for Young Negotiators, Inc., Cambridge, Massachusetts.

and essential to effective communication. The PYN course emphasizes the futility of adversarial aggression and the utility of collaboration.

The Peace Education Foundation

The Peace Education Foundation (PEF), based in Miami, Florida, offers a grade-level-specific, classroom-tested curriculum for prekindergarten through grade 12.[2] The curriculum has a unified scope, sequence of content, and sequence of skills. PEF views conflict resolution as a body of knowledge and skills that equips individuals with the ability to use a nonviolent, constructive approach when dealing with life's inevitable conflicts. PEF focuses on children and the adults who facilitate children's social, emotional, and intellectual growth. Since much of this growth occurs in schools, PEF's goals are to make schools safe and more disciplined, improve school climate, make instructional strategies more effective, and foster resiliency in children. To make conflict resolution "standard operating

procedure" in schools, PEF programs are purposefully linked to school improvement and related initiatives.

The content of the PEF conflict resolution curriculum encompasses a range of social competency skills that are grouped into five components:

◆ **Community building:** Establishing trust, exploring common interests, and respecting differences.

◆ **Understanding conflict:** Identifying conflict, the elements of conflict, escalation and deescalation, and different conflict management styles.

◆ **Perception:** Understanding different points of view, enhancing empathy, and increasing tolerance.

◆ **Anger management:** Understanding the pros and cons of anger, anger triggers, and anger styles; increasing tolerance for frustration; and learning anger management plans.

♦ **Rules for Fighting Fair:** Learning the rules that provide a framework for appropriate behavior and the associated skills, such as identifying and focusing on the problem; attacking the problem, not the person; listening with an open mind; treating a person's feelings with respect; and taking responsibility for one's actions.

These rules are central to the PEF conflict resolution program because they are the principles of nonviolent conflict resolution that promote a peaceful, disciplined environment. The rules also provide a constructive alternative to "fouls"—inappropriate behaviors that attack the dignity of others and escalate conflict, such as putting the other down, being sarcastic, bringing up the past, hitting, not taking responsibility, getting even, not listening, and making excuses. All PEF curriculums include an age-appropriate poster of the rules, a helpful visual reminder for all members of the school community.

Once the rules have been mastered, more sophisticated content and skills from the PEF components can be added to enhance students' social competency. These additional components include affirming self-identity, refusing peer pressure, acting in a self-empowering way, dealing with bullies, establishing self-control, setting goals, acting with courage and conviction, understanding violence, having healthy relationships with boyfriends/girlfriends, and being a peacemaker.

Teachers facilitate the process of the PEF conflict resolution curriculum by using five strategies:

♦ **Model:** Profess the attitudes expected of students and practice the associated behaviors. The goal is to let students know how, in "real life," to use the Rules for Fighting Fair and skills such as reflective listening, "I" statements, and problem solving.

♦ **Teach:** Teach the students what to do and why. Break the skills into understandable parts and give them the chance to practice through role-play. The goal is for students to learn the techniques so they can repeat the vocabulary and techniques when prompted.

♦ **Coach:** Assist students in using the techniques appropriately in real-life situations. Offer support and corrective feedback when needed. The goal is for students to practice what they have learned.

♦ **Encourage:** Remind students to use their skills. Express confidence in their ability to succeed. Recognize students' appropriate use of skills. The goal is for students to behave appropriately without depending on adults.

♦ **Delegate:** After students become proficient, let them teach or coach less experienced students. The goal is for students to demonstrate their competence and acknowledge the value of habitual use of the skills.

Mediation

Schools report that, as the number of students and adults skilled in mediation increases in a school, the incidence of conflict in the school decreases. The mediation curriculum, therefore, is the next step in a well-implemented conflict resolution program. The PEF program includes mediation curriculums for grades 4 though 7 and 8 through 12.[3] These curriculums provide step-by-step instructions for training peer mediators and monitoring a school-based mediation program.

Parent Involvement

Parent involvement in and support for a school-based conflict resolution program is critical. PEF's text *Fighting Fair for Families* offers families a chance to reinforce conflict resolution at home.[4] The text covers communication skills, anger management techniques, and basic mediation skills in English, Spanish, French, and Haitian Creole.

PEF has devised a variety of implementation models that can be used in a classroom, school, or school district. PEF conflict resolution components may be incorporated into traditional academic lessons. In addition, the conflict resolution components or specific PEF curriculum lessons may be taught with subject areas. Drop Everything for Peace is a PEF approach that sets aside time on a regular basis to teach only PEF components and curriculums.

National Institute for Citizen Education in the Law

To promote cooperation instead of competition, the National Institute for Citizen Education in the Law (NICEL), a grantee of the Office of Juvenile Justice and Delinquency Prevention (OJJDP), has interwoven strategies for conflict management and mediation into many of its programs and curriculum materials. NICEL's text *Street Law: A Course in Practical Law* is used in schools, juvenile justice settings, and communities nationwide and has been adapted for use in other countries.[5]

Middle and High School Programs and Curricular Materials

In 1985, NICEL, in partnership with the National Crime Prevention Council (NCPC), formed the Teens, Crime, and the Community (TCC) program, which is funded by OJJDP. The TCC program helps teens understand how crime affects them and their families, friends, and communities, and involves them in a service focused on making their communities safer. Conflict management lessons are a key student activity. This program includes

> I learned how to keep calm and keep the disputants calm—to help them solve their problems and not to solve the problem for them.
>
> *Student, North Carolina*

comprehensive program design, teacher and community resource training and preparation, and student and teacher materials development.

With funding from OJJDP, NICEL and NCPC produced conflict resolution education curriculums designed for specific student audiences: *We Can Work It Out! Problem Solving Through Mediation* (elementary and secondary school editions) and *The Conflict Zoo*. *We Can Work It Out! Problem Solving Through Mediation* for secondary schools involves a step-by-step design to teach the skills of personal conflict management and the process of mediation.[6] Through these lessons, teachers can impart valuable skills in analytical reasoning, active listening, patience, empathy, and generating opinions. The curriculum teaches students key terms and concepts and allows them to learn experientially. Students apply the skills they learn in scenarios in which they assume the roles of disputants and mediators.

An outgrowth of *We Can Work It Out!* is the Mediation Showcase. NICEL, in partnership with the National Institute for Dispute Resolution (NIDR), designed mediation showcases to popularize conflict management skills. At these showcases, students are given conflict scenarios where they role-play the disputants and mediators. Community resource people, including community mediators and other volunteers who use skills involved in conflict management, provide feedback to the students on their ability to resolve the conflicts presented to them. This forum provides an opportunity for students to celebrate their newly learned skills and interact with adults in a constructive and affirming environment. In turn, these events provide an excellent opportunity for authentic assessment.

Elementary Programs and Curricular Materials

After its initial secondary school curriculum, NICEL developed two elementary curriculums. *The Conflict Zoo* is a curriculum for the third and fourth grades designed to teach the building blocks of conflict resolution and the concepts of justice and fairness.[7] The lessons are given at the beginning of the school year to help students understand conflict management and develop fair rules to live by. The lessons begin with the story of a junior zoo where baby animals play together. To do this, the baby animals must resolve their conflicts nonviolently and build a sense of community. The students experience these everyday conflicts through the eyes of the animals. The philosophy, principles, and skills of conflict resolution are interwoven in role-plays about junior zoo conflicts. Students gradually move from helping the animals resolve their conflicts to resolving conflicts in their own lives. Over the course of the lessons, children learn important terms, create journals, and apply these new ideas to their lives. Role-plays, art, and journal keeping are used to keep the children interested and provide ways for them to internalize and apply the skills they learn in a range of situations.

Another curriculum, *We Can Work It Out! Problem Solving Through Mediation* for elementary schools, follows the same format as *We Can Work It Out!* for secondary schools, except that the terminology used and the scenarios created are appropriate for elementary school students.[8] Elementary mediation showcases parallel the secondary ones described above. Scenarios for students often involve fairy tales, cartoons, and interpersonal conflicts.

Process Curriculum in Juvenile Justice Settings

NICEL's lessons for juvenile justice settings focus on developing an understanding of practical law. Life skills like anger management, communication, and the problem-solving processes of conflict resolution are at the heart of every lesson. The interactive strategies and real-world scenarios keep participants engaged in applying newly learned information. NICEL provides training and materials for juvenile justice professionals in prevention, intervention, and youth development under an OJJDP grant.

> I learned that you can work out problems without going to the principal's office.
>
> *Student, North Carolina*

NICEL programs can be used separately or integrated into existing curriculums and programs. Schools that have a peer mediation program can use the *We Can Work It Out!* curriculum to extend the philosophy and skills to the rest of the school population. If a school has not yet developed a conflict resolution education program, a logical first step might be to teach the philosophy and skills of conflict resolution to the entire school community and then to set up a mediation program. The use of these programs and curriculums can help develop a corps of trained practitioners in the school community who have the skills to handle everyday conflicts.

Notes

1. Curhan, J.R. 1996. *Life Negotiations: The PYN Curriculum for Middle Schools.* Cambridge, MA: Program for Young Negotiators, Inc.

2. Some of the curriculums available from PEF are *Peacemaking Skills for Little Kids, Pre K–K* (F. Schmidt and A. Friedman, 1993), *Peacemaking Skills for Little Kids, Grade One* (D. Berkell, K. Kotzen, and S. Rizzo, 1996), *Peacemaking Skills for Little Kids, Grade Two* (E. Brunt, A. Friedman, F. Schmidt, and T. Solotoff, 1996), *Peace Scholars: Learning Through Literature, Grade Three* (D. Carlebach, 1996), *Creative Conflict Solving for Kids, Grade Four* (F. Schmidt and A. Friedman, 1991), *Creative Conflict Solving for Kids, Grade Five* (F. Schmidt and A. Friedman, 1985), *Creating Peace, Building Community, Grade Six* (J. Bachoy, 1996), and *Creating Peace, Building Community, Grade Seven* (J. Bachoy, 1996). For more information on these curriculums, see the section "Process Curriculum" in appendix B.

3. The PEF mediation curriculums include *Mediation for Kids* (F. Schmidt, A. Friedman, and J. Marvel, 1992) and *Mediation: Getting to Win/Win!* (F. Schmidt and J. Burke, 1994). For more information on these curriculums, see the section "Mediation" in appendix B.

4. Schmidt, F., and A. Friedman. 1994. *Fighting Fair for Families.* Miami, FL: Peace 10 Education Foundation.

5. Arbetman, L.P., E.T. McMahon, and E.L. O'Brien. 1994. *Street Law: A Course in Practical Law*, 5th edition. St. Paul, MN: West Publishing Company.

6. Glickman, S., and J. Zimmer. 1993. *We Can Work It Out!: Problem Solving Through Mediation, Secondary Edition.* Washington, DC: National Institute for Citizen Education in the Law. See "Process Curriculum," appendix B, for more information.

7. Glickman, S., N. Johnson, G. Sirianni, and J. Zimmer. 1996. *The Conflict Zoo.* Washington, DC: National Institute for Citizen Education in the Law. See "Process Curriculum," appendix B, for more information.

8. Barnes-Robinson, L., S. Jewler, and J. Zimmer. 1996. *We Can Work It Out!: Problem Solving Through Mediation, Elementary Edition.* Washington, DC: National Institute for Citizen Education in the Law. See "Process Curriculum," appendix B, for more information.

Chapter 3: Mediation Program Approach

Mediation Program: A conflict resolution education program in which selected individuals (adults and/or students) are trained in the principles and foundation abilities of conflict resolution and in the mediation process in order to provide neutral third-party facilitation to assist those in conflict to reach a resolution.

The mediation process is a mechanism for resolving conflicts that can be used within schools, the community, youth-serving organizations, and juvenile justice settings. Within these settings, mediation programs are established to:

◆ Reduce the number of disciplinary actions, such as detentions, suspensions, and lockdowns.

◆ Encourage more effective problem solving.

◆ Reduce the time adults or youth leaders spend dealing with conflicts between youth.

◆ Improve school or agency climate.

◆ Provide youth and staff with an alternative forum for problem solving.

Mediation programs can help manage and resolve conflicts between young people, between young people and adults, and between adults. The principal, teachers, or other adults can be trained as mediators to help young people and adults resolve their disputes. For example, an adult mediator can assist adults in resolving conflicts such as work problems between staff members, disciplinary actions disputed by parents, and disputes over the development of appropriate programs for children with special needs.

Youth mediators help resolve disputes between peers involving jealousies, rumors, misunderstandings, bullying, fights, personal property, and

We help kids who are fighting talk about their problems. Some people think kids can't help other kids solve their problems. But we can. It's real neat because we don't work out things for kids who are fighting. They solve their own problems and we help.

Fourth-grade mediator, Wilmette, Illinois

damaged friendships. In addition, youth and adults may co-mediate conflicts such as personality clashes, issues of respect and behavior, and other conflicts that damage youth-adult relationships. Youth-adult mediations are usually an outgrowth of established peer mediation programs or adult mediation programs.

The Mediation Process

Mediation is a process in which one or more mediators serve as neutral facilitators to help disputants negotiate an agreement. In this process, the mediator creates and maintains an environment that fosters mutual problem solving. During mediation, the mediator uses the six problem-solving steps of conflict resolution:

◆ Set the stage—establish ground rules for problem solving.

◆ Gather perspectives—listen to each disputant's point of view.

◆ Identify interests contributing to the conflict.

◆ Create options that address the interests of both disputants.

- Evaluate these options according to objective criteria.

- Generate an agreement satisfactory to each disputant.

Although the mediator controls the process, the disputants control the outcome. Participation in mediation is voluntary, and the mediator does not judge, impose an agreement, or force a solution. Mediation is powerful because conflicts can only be resolved if the disputants choose to resolve them. Disputants can judge best what will resolve the conflict and are more likely to execute the terms of an agreement if they have authored them.

Peer Mediation Programs

Peer mediation programs are among the most widely chosen types of conflict resolution programs in schools. Young people can become effective mediators because they understand their peers, make the process age appropriate, empower their peers and command their respect, and normalize the conflict resolution process.[1]

Young people can connect with their peers in ways that adults cannot. Peer mediators can frame disputes in the perspective, language, and attitudes of youth. Young people perceive peer mediation as a way to talk out problems without the fear of an adult judging their behavior, thoughts, or feelings. Peer mediators are respected because they uphold the problem-solving process and honor the disputants in the way they conduct the mediation sessions. The self-empowering process appeals to youth and fosters self-esteem and self-discipline. When young people solve their own problems, they feel they are in control and can make a commitment to the solutions they have created.

Peer Mediation Training

In schoolwide peer mediation programs, a cadre of students is trained in conflict resolution. Peer mediation training is flexible and accommodates the school's schedule and resources and the developmental level of the students involved. For example, training for elementary students might be conducted in 2-hour sessions over several weeks, whereas training for high school students might be done in full-day sessions. Peer mediation training takes a minimum of 12 to 20 hours with ongoing opportunities to develop the skills of the mediators (see table 1).

Respect for diversity and cultural competency are also taught to peer mediators. Incorporating simulations with cross-cultural themes and social justice issues into training activities effectively prepares peer mediators for conflicts deriving from diversity.

Developing skill in the mediation process is a life-long activity. Peer mediators are encouraged to practice and use their training in conflict resolution as often as possible and to take refresher classes.

Peer Mediation Opportunity

Peer mediation programs offer all young people constructive means of resolving conflicts. Peer mediators who are properly trained acquire and internalize conflict resolution skills that can benefit them in many different ways throughout their lives. For this reason, many experts believe that peer mediation programs should be implemented not as a solitary entity, but as an integral part of a total school conflict resolution program that offers mediators and others the opportunity to develop conflict resolution skills. In the following sections, two mediation programs are described.

Peer Mediation in Schools Program From the New Mexico Center for Dispute Resolution

The Peer Mediation in Schools Program developed by the New Mexico Center for Dispute Resolution (NMCDR) is designed to train staff and the entire student body in the mediation process, with selected students trained as peer mediators. The program has three components—teacher modeling, a curriculum, and mediation—and is intended for use in a wide range of contexts and settings, which are described in detail on the following pages.

Table 1: Recommended Time for Peer Mediation Training

Grade Level	Minimum Number of Hours of Training
Elementary school	12–16
Middle school	12–16
High school	15–20

Source: National Association for Mediation in Education. 1995. *Standards for Peer Mediation Programs.* Washington, DC: National Institute for Dispute Resolution.

Teacher Modeling

The program's success depends on the support and commitment of the entire school staff. At an orientation meeting, staff are presented with several options. They can:

♦ Pledge general support for the program.

♦ Refer students to mediation and encourage participation in the process.

♦ Agree to participate in mediation with a student if appropriate.

♦ Take part in conflict resolution training if training is offered at the school.

♦ Participate in mediation training and serve as a staff mediator.

♦ Serve as a member of the mediation implementation team.

♦ Serve as a program coordinator.

In any of these roles, teachers demonstrate the value and importance of problem solving and communication by applying these skills in the classroom, the hallway, the office, and in interactions with colleagues and with parents.

Curriculum Component

Teaching the curriculum is mandatory at the elementary level and optional at the middle and secondary levels. At the elementary level, the curriculum is designed to teach and reinforce communication, develop vocabulary and concepts related to conflict, and develop problem-solving skills. Two manuals are used: *Resolving Conflict: Activities for Grades K–3* and *Lessons in Conflict Resolution for Grades 4–6.*[2] The curriculum is used in all class settings, allowing all students to develop conflict resolution skills. At the secondary level, a 15-lesson curriculum, *Managing Conflict: A Curriculum for Adolescents*, is used in homeroom and social studies, civics, language, and English classes.[3] The curriculum teaches and reinforces skills in communication, problem solving, and anger management.

Mediation Component

Selection of peer mediators is similar at the elementary, middle, and secondary levels. Students and staff nominate potential mediators, and a committee of teachers makes the final selection based on a balance of "negative" and "positive" factors. Selected staff and students are then trained in the mediation process.

At the elementary level, selected mediators from grades 4 through 6 receive an additional 9 hours of training after they complete the mediation curriculum. After a publicized graduation ceremony, student mediators in teams of two watch the playground for developing conflicts and offer their help in resolving them. Some schools also use a classroom referral system. The NMCDR *Training and Implementation Guide for Student Mediation in Elementary Schools* provides a detailed description of program implementation.[4]

At the secondary level, selected teacher and student mediators receive 12 hours of training after they complete the mediation curriculum. After training, students and staff refer conflicts to the program coordinator for mediation; participation is voluntary. Disputes between two students are handled by a team of two student mediators, and disputes between a staff member and a student are handled by a student and staff mediator team. The NMCDR *Training and Implementation Guide for Student Mediation in Secondary Schools* contains information on training mediators and implementing the program.[5]

> I have been through student-teacher mediation this semester and found it to be a positive, equitable method of achieving conflict resolution. The student and I had repeated confrontations about attitude and academic performance. Through the mediation the student felt more at ease— less pressured. I became aware of my own actions and his concerns and modified my behavior accordingly. The student has become less disruptive and confrontational.
>
> *Teacher, Ortiz Middle School*

NMCDR initially conducts district staff orientation workshops to discuss the philosophical and organizational realities of conflict resolution. Thereafter, NMCDR and the school district enter into an agreement that specifies the responsibilities of each party. NMCDR's responsibilities are to:

♦ Help create district implementation teams composed of teachers, parents, community youth workers, juvenile probation officers, and students.

♦ Provide onsite training; each district receives a number of service days based on the district team's plan.

♦ Provide technical assistance that includes training students and staff in mediation and conflict resolution skills; giving presentations to school board members, parents, administrators, and

staff to build program support; planning program development; providing program management assistance to district team members and school program coordinators; and providing other assistance identified by the district.

♦ Supply implementation manuals and curriculum materials with permission to duplicate as needed for the school district's use.

♦ Work on site with the district team to assess district needs, exchange information that defines services to be provided, plan strategies for problem-solving or development activities, develop long-term plans for program implementation, and mentor district trainers for up to 2 years.

♦ Conduct an annual evaluation examining the strengths and weaknesses of all new and ongoing NMCDR programs.

The school district's responsibilities over a period of 3 to 5 years are to:

♦ Maintain a district implementation team that includes a district-level administrator and community members and meets at least twice a year.

♦ Maintain programs at all schools where a program has been implemented.

♦ Provide substitute and inservice time for staff and coordinator training.

♦ Develop a written plan that includes a 3- to 5-year plan and goals for districtwide expansion, annual district goals, and a list of services needed for the year.

♦ Identify new schools for program implementation in the following academic year.

♦ Maintain originals of curriculum materials and mediation training manuals provided by NMCDR and provide and distribute copies to schools.

♦ Select four to six candidates to be trained as internal district trainers and provide support such as release time and substitute salary to allow them to train within the district.

- Support programs during transitions (e.g., during changes of staff).

- Establish policies for mediation programs.

- Integrate mediation into the schools' and the district's disciplinary policies.

- Build connections with the community, including private and public agencies such as juvenile probation and social services.

By training educators to become conflict resolution trainers, NMCDR helps districts become independent, thereby ensuring a smooth transfer of responsibility. The district trainers assume responsibility for creating and maintaining mediation and conflict resolution programs and for conducting training in the schools. At that point, NMCDR staff withdraw from the school district's program.

Illinois Institute for Dispute Resolution

The Illinois Institute for Dispute Resolution (IIDR) implements and operates its peer mediation program in six developmental phases (figure 3). During the first phase, the conflict resolution program team is created and trained, the program coordinators are designated, a needs assessment is conducted, and faculty consensus for program development is built. IIDR is actively involved with the school or district in this phase, providing technical assistance and training for the program team. Throughout all six phases, IIDR provides technical assistance to the program team, including first-time training to other staff, community members, parents, and student peer mediators. In any of these trainings conducted by IIDR, program team members always participate and provide followup training after the program's first year.

> We need to face the reality that what we are doing is not working. We must do something different. This is different and I believe it will work!
>
> *Assistant principal, Chicago, Illinois*

> My first-grade son came home the other day and told me, "Mom, I have a problem with Jessica. We need to talk." I came in to ask the teacher what was going on because he usually says that she's mean and he hates her. I was excited about the change in his way of talking. The teacher told me he was having a class in conflict resolution.
>
> *Parent, Bayard Elementary School*

Phase I: Develop the Program Team and Commitment

A peer mediation program must be perceived as fulfilling the needs of both faculty and students. A broad-based coalition of administrators, classroom teachers, special educators, counselors, deans, social workers, and health educators interested in developing a conflict resolution program is necessary for a successful program. This team may also include parents, students, or community members. The team is the key to a successful program because the members initiate the program and are charged with gaining the support of the entire school staff.

After the team is formed, it must build its capacity to develop a quality peer mediation program. The program team must be trained to become informed decisionmakers, effective implementers, and strong advocates for the program. Since the program team will be responsible for the supervision and training of student mediators, the team members must be trained in the principles of conflict resolution and mediation and methods for mediation training. Content for the training includes:

- Understanding conflict.

- Principles of conflict resolution.

- Social and cultural diversity and conflict resolution.

- Mediation process and skills.

- Program organization and operation.

- Role of peer mediation in the school.

- Rationale for peer mediation.

Figure 3: The Six Developmental Phases of the Mediation Program of the Illinois Institute for Dispute Resolution

Phase I: **Develop the Program Team and Commitment**
- Create program team.
- Train program team.
- Designate program coordinators.
- Conduct needs assessment.
- Build faculty consensus for program development.

Phase II: **Design and Plan the Program**
- Develop timeline for implementation.
- Establish advisory committee.
- Develop policies and procedures.
- Identify and develop funding sources.

Phase III: **Select and Train the Mediators**
- Conduct student orientation.
- Select peer mediators.
- Train mediators.
- Recognize peer mediators.

Phase IV: **Educate a Critical Mass**
- Conduct faculty inservice training.
- Conduct student workshops.
- Provide family and community orientation.
- Offer parent workshops.

Phase V: **Develop and Execute a Promotional Campaign**
- Execute initial campaign.
- Develop ongoing promotion.

Phase VI: **Program Operation and Maintenance**
- Request mediation process.
- Schedule mediations and mediators.
- Supervise mediation session.
- Provide mediators ongoing training and support.
- Evaluate program.

Source: Schrumpf, F., D. Crawford, and R. Bodine. 1996. *Peer Mediation: Conflict Resolution in Schools.* Revised edition. Champaign, IL: Research Press, Inc. Reprinted with permission of the authors and Research Press.

> Mediation met a deep-seated need. . . .
> Conflict is resolved on a verbal level and
> does not get to the physical. . . . Peer
> mediation teaches that different is not
> necessarily bad. . . . We tend to realize
> that the other person is just like us.
>
> *Teacher, Rockford, Illinois*

IIDR believes that trainers should have mediation experience. The team members should therefore be involved in mediation training and continue to increase their skills through practice.

During phase I the program coordinators are designated. The effectiveness of the peer mediation program is strongly linked to the quality of program coordinators, who are responsible for the ongoing organization and operation of the peer mediation program and must personify the conflict resolution principles they promote. Program coordinators:

- ◆ Facilitate the program team in designing and planning the peer mediation program.

- ◆ Plan and conduct orientation sessions for faculty, students, families, and the community.

- ◆ Coordinate the selection of peer mediators and the training of students.

- ◆ Establish and facilitate the advisory committee.

- ◆ Promote the program.

- ◆ Receive requests for mediation and schedule mediators and mediations.

- ◆ Arrange for supervision of mediators and provide for ongoing mediator training and support.

- ◆ Facilitate ongoing communication with the program team.

- ◆ Develop parent and community participation.

- ◆ Collect mediation data and evaluate the program.

This phase also includes a needs assessment conducted to establish school and community support for a conflict resolution program. Broad-based support is essential to sustaining a school conflict resolution program. Faculty consensus on the program's development must also be built. Without shared vision among faculty, the program will not grow and is not likely to survive.

Phase II: Design and Plan the Program

Following phase I, IIDR encourages the school to establish an advisory committee of 10 to 12 members representing the varied interests of the school and community, including parents, teachers, school and district administrators, students, support staff, community representatives, and corporate sponsors. The advisory committee oversees the development of the program, including the role of mediation within the school's discipline program; assists the program team in developing timelines for implementation; and identifies and develops funding sources.

> The training was great. . . . Everybody left
> the training so enthused and committed to
> developing the program. . . . Never before
> had anything been done districtwide, and
> we wanted to do it with this type of pro-
> gram so the students would get the same
> message across grades. . . . We had a vision
> that we could make this work in Freeport.
>
> *Counselor and program team member,*
> *Freeport, Illinois*

Phase III: Select and Train the Mediators

Phase III encompasses recruiting, selecting, and training student mediators. IIDR suggests that nominations be broadly solicited from staff and students, including self-nominations. Several processes may be used to select mediators, but IIDR believes that one of the more effective is a lottery. Selection by lottery is preferable because interested students will take the risk of applying when they do not fear rejection. It is also important that students not have a negative experience with the peer mediation program. Lottery selection is perceived as an opportunity, whereas selection by criteria can be perceived as a personal risk. A student rejected as a peer mediator may reject the mediation process if he or she later experiences a conflict. This attitude can potentially spread from one individual to groups of peers, who would then also refuse to participate in the mediation. The lottery must also provide for the proper representation of the school's diverse groups if it is to work well.

> **Even some of the tougher kids are starting to see fighting as pretty stupid.**
>
> *Middle school mediator, Champaign, Illinois*

The IIDR program for student mediation training involves 12 to 15 hours of basic training and 12 to 15 hours of additional advanced training. The basic training activities include understanding conflict, responses to conflict, sources of conflict, communication skills, the role of the mediator, and the mediation process. The advanced training includes bias awareness, social/cultural diversity, advanced communication, uncovering hidden interests, dealing with anger, caucusing, negotiation, and group problem solving.

Students who complete the basic training can mediate most disputes between peers. The advanced training strengthens their abilities to use the mediation process and expands their understanding of diversity with regard to conflict resolution.

Phase IV: Educate a Critical Mass

The fourth phase of the program focuses on educating a critical mass about conflict, conflict resolution, and the mediation process via workshops for faculty, students, parents, and the community. In the IIDR program, the staff inservice training is a minimum of 6 hours. The purpose of the inservice training is to help the staff develop a common understanding of conflict, learn the principles of conflict resolution, develop an understanding of the mediation process, learn how to support the development of the peer mediation program through curriculum integration and referral of conflicts to mediation, and prepare to conduct student workshops.

Workshops for students last about 5 hours and are designed to develop an understanding of conflict, peace, and peacemaking; communication and negotiation skills; and an understanding of peer mediation and procedures for requesting peer mediation services. Student peer mediators are often used to provide orientation programs for and assist in training faculty, students, parents, and community groups.

Phase V: Develop and Execute a Promotional Campaign

The fifth phase consists of developing and executing a promotional campaign. Like many new ideas, peer mediation can be greeted with skepticism. Students may be reluctant to try a new approach. Many students may feel as if they are backing down or losing face if they talk problems through. Promoting the program among the student population is crucial to its success, but the campaign activities must be revived periodically and continue through the life of the program.

> **There are so many more problems today that they naturally affect our kids. They need ways to deal with their own problems.**
>
> *Parent, Chicago, Illinois*

Phase VI: Program Operation and Maintenance

Phase VI encompasses every aspect of program operation and maintenance—requesting mediation scheduling mediations and mediators, supervising mediators, recording mediation data, providing ongoing training and support, and evaluating programs. Conducting a program evaluation builds a solid case for ongoing support for peer mediation and provides information to improve the program and change the school system.

> I don't have nearly the number of conflicts to deal with as I used to. A referral must be pretty serious now for it to come to me. My playground supervisors also see a big difference. School peacemakers (peer mediators) aren't enough. Mediation must get into the classrooms.
>
> *Principal, Mt. Carmel, Illinois*

IIDR promotes peer mediation as a way to establish conflict resolution programs in schools and works with schools in the process of developing and implementing peer mediation programs to extend conflict resolution training to a broader constituency within the school than the few who are trained as peer mediators.[6]

Notes

1. Cohen, R. 1995. *Students Resolving Conflict: Peer Mediation in Schools*. Glenview, IL: GoodYear Books, pp. 44–45.

2. Copeland, N., and F. Garfield. 1989. *Resolving Conflict: Activities for Grades K–3*. Albuquerque, NM: New Mexico Center for Dispute Resolution. *Lessons in Conflict Resolution for Grades 4–6*. 1994. Albuquerque, NM: New Mexico Center for Dispute Resolution. For more information on both curriculums, see "Mediation," appendix B.

3. Copeland, N.D., and M. Smith (editors). 1989. *Managing Conflict: A Curriculum for Adolescents*. Albuquerque, NM: New Mexico Center for Dispute Resolution. For more information, see "Mediation" in appendix B.

4. Keeney, S., and J. Sidwell. 1990. *Training and Implementation Guide for Student Mediation in Elementary Schools*. Albuquerque, NM: New Mexico Center for Dispute Resolution. For more information, see the section "Mediation" in appendix B.

5. Smith, M., and J. Sidwell. 1990. *Training and Implementation Guide for Student Mediation in Secondary Schools*. Albuquerque, NM: New Mexico Center for Dispute Resolution. For more information, see "Mediation," appendix B.

6. Schrumpf, F., D. Crawford, and R. Bodine. 1996. *Peer Mediation: Conflict Resolution in Schools*. Revised edition. Champaign, IL: Research Press, Inc.

Chapter 4: Peaceable Classroom Approach

Peaceable Classroom: A whole-classroom methodology that includes teaching students the foundation abilities, principles, and one or more of the three problem-solving processes of conflict resolution. Conflict resolution education is incorporated into the core subjects of the curriculum and into classroom management strategies. Peaceable classrooms are the building blocks of the peaceable school.

Peaceable classrooms are initiated on a teacher-by-teacher basis. The peaceable classroom approach integrates conflict resolution into the curriculum and into the management of the classroom and uses the instructional methods of cooperative learning and academic controversy.

Curriculum Integration and Classroom Management

Curriculum integration occurs when the skills and concepts needed to resolve conflicts constructively are incorporated into core subject areas. Teachers who integrate conflict resolution into their curriculums help create classroom environments that support conflict resolution and prosocial behavior. William Kreidler, a pioneer of the peaceable classroom, views the classroom as a caring and respectful community having five qualities: cooperation, communication, emotional expression, appreciation for diversity, and conflict resolution.[1] Peaceable classrooms incorporate learning activities and teachable moments that encourage youth to recognize and choose nonviolent options in conflict situations, meet the needs of the individuals involved, and improve relationships.

Each of us must be the change we want to see in the world.

Mahatma Gandhi

Cooperative Learning and Academic Controversy

Teachers in peaceable classrooms extensively use the cooperative learning and academic controversy methods developed by David Johnson and Roger Johnson. In cooperative learning, students work in small groups to accomplish shared learning goals. Students have the responsibility to learn the assigned material and ensure that other group members learn it.[2] Academic controversy methods are used when one student's ideas, information, conclusions, theories, and opinions are incompatible with those of another and the two seek to reach an agreement. Controversies are resolved through deliberate discourse—the discussion of the advantages and disadvantages of proposed actions. Such discussion is aimed at creative problem solving by synthesizing novel solutions.[3]

In peaceable classrooms, youth learn to take responsibility for their actions and develop a sense of connectedness to others and their environment. Peaceable classrooms build the capacity of youth to manage and resolve conflict on their own by learning to:

♦ Understand and analyze conflict.

♦ Understand peace and peacemaking.

♦ Recognize the role of perceptions and biases.

- Identify feelings.

- Identify factors that cause escalation.

- Handle anger and other feelings appropriately.

- Improve listening skills.

- Improve verbal communication skills.

- Identify common interests.

- Brainstorm multiple options that address interests.

- Evaluate the consequences of different options.

- Create a win-win agreement.

The Ohio Commission on Dispute Resolution's *Conflict Management Resource Guide for Elementary Schools* suggests the following ways to incorporate conflict and conflict resolution into the core areas of the curriculum:[4]

- **Art:** Study contrast, perspective, and feeling in the production or study of art.

- **Health:** Recognize and evaluate the consequences of unhealthy behavior and brainstorm alternative choices.

- **Language Arts:**

  ◇ *Reading:* Analyze factual or fictional stories to identify the causes of conflicts and their solutions while discussing additional options for resolving them.

  ◇ *Writing:* Use story starters to provide opportunities for students to think about and apply conflict resolution skills in their creative writing.

- **Mathematics:** Ask students to develop a plan for a city park that meets a variety of community interests and budget constraints.

- **Music:** Reinforce the principles of harmony and discord and their similarity to the problem-solving processes of conflict resolution.

- **Physical Education:** Discuss the differences between competitive and cooperative games and ground rules that encourage or discourage a peaceful sports climate.

- **Science:** Discuss and analyze the symbiotic relationships found in nature.

- **Social Studies:** Analyze past or present local, State, national, and international conflicts and discuss various conflict resolution strategies to resolve them.

The Educators for Social Responsibility (ESR) curriculum *Making Choices About Conflict, Security, and Peacemaking* offers other examples for incorporating conflict resolution into primary and supplementary lessons for the secondary level:[5]

- **Literature:** Explore the concept of conflict escalation in novels and short stories, or read selections about American and global peacemakers whose life work has made a positive difference for others, for example, Eleanor Roosevelt, Cesar Chavez, Mary McLeod Bethune, Ralph Bunche, and Jane Addams.

- **Science:** Introduce the concept of global ecology by examining environmental problems that require international cooperation.

- **Civics:** Explore tools of public policy and political pressure that are employed at local, State, national, and international levels. Study State and Federal legislation or international policies on controversial issues.

- **Introduction to the Law:** Explore the tuna fish controversy (drift net fishing and the Law of the Seas) as a way to understand the impact of change in the law on local and national economies and international relations.

- **World Geography:** Compare different nations to identify how geographic features influence economy and quality of life.

- **American History:** Study the successes and failures of international peacekeeping in the 20th century, specifically contrasting the League of Nations and the United Nations.

Two examples of peaceable classroom programs follow.

Teaching Students To Be Peacemakers Program

The Teaching Students To Be Peacemakers (TSP) program offered by the Cooperative Learning Center of the University of Minnesota is a 12-year spiral program for schools in which students learn increasingly sophisticated negotiation and mediation procedures each year.[6] In the TSP program, the school's faculty create a cooperative environment, teach students to be peacemakers, implement the peacemaker program, and refine and upgrade the students' skills.

Faculty Create a Cooperative Environment

Cooperative learning creates a context for the constructive resolution of conflicts. It also reduces the factors that place students at risk for using violence, such as poor academic performance (with an inability to think decisions through) and alienation from schoolmates. Cooperative learning, compared with competitive or individualistic learning, results in higher academic achievement and increased use of higher level reasoning strategies, more caring and supportive relationships, and greater self-esteem.

Faculty Teach Students To Be Peacemakers

Under TSP, all students receive 30 minutes of training per day for approximately 30 days and then 30 minutes of training approximately twice a week for the rest of the school year. The training includes:

- **Understanding the Nature of Conflict.** Learning includes recognizing conflicts by focusing attention on problems, clarifying disputants' values, revealing how disputants need to change, increasing higher level cognitive and moral reasoning, increasing motivation to learn, providing insights into other perspectives and life experiences, strengthening relationships, adding fun and variety to life, and increasing disputants' ability to cope with stress and be resilient in the face of adversity.

- **Choosing an Appropriate Conflict Strategy.** Students, faculty, and administrators learn that they have two concerns when facing a conflict:

achieving their goals and maintaining a good relationship with the other person. The balance between the two determines whether they should:

- ◇ **Withdraw,** giving up both the goals and the relationship.

- ◇ **Force,** achieving the goal at the other person's expense, thereby giving up the relationship.

- ◇ **Smooth,** giving up the goal to enhance the relationship.

- ◇ **Compromise,** giving up part of the goal at some damage to the relationship.

- ◇ **Negotiate,** solving the problem, thus achieving the goal and maintaining the relationship.

Participants are taught that in long-term relationships, such as those with schoolmates and faculty, the most important strategy is the problem-solving process of negotiation.

- **Negotiating To Solve the Problem.** It is not enough to tell students to "be nice," or "talk it out," or "solve your problem." They must be taught specific procedures for resolving conflicts. This part of the training teaches students, faculty, and administrators specific procedures for negotiating agreements that result in all disputants achieving their goals while maintaining or even improving the quality of their relationships (see figure 4).

- **Mediating Others' Conflicts.** Participants are taught the four-step mediation procedure:

- ◇ **Ending hostilities.** The mediator ensures that disputants end hostilities and cool off. If the disputants are too angry to solve their problems, they must cool down before mediation begins.

- ◇ **Ensuring disputants are committed to the mediation process.** The mediator introduces the process of mediation and sets the ground rules.

- ◇ **Helping disputants successfully negotiate with each other.** The mediator carefully takes the disputants through the negotiation procedure.

Figure 4: The Problem-Solving Negotiation Procedure

Describe what you want. *"I want to use the book now."* This involves using good communication skills and defining the conflict as a small and specific mutual problem.

Describe how you feel. *"I'm frustrated."* Disputants must understand how they feel and communicate it accurately and unambiguously.

Describe the reasons for your wants and feelings. *"You have been using the book for the past hour. If I don't get to use the book soon, my report will not be done on time. It's frustrating to have to wait so long."* This step includes expressing cooperative intentions, listening carefully, separating interests from positions, and differentiating before trying to integrate the two sets of interests.

Take the other's perspective and summarize your understanding of what the other person wants, how the other person feels, and the reasons underlying both. *"My understanding of you is . . . ."* This includes understanding the perspective of the opposing disputant and being able to see the problem from both perspectives simultaneously.

Invent three optional plans to resolve the conflict that maximize joint benefits. *"Plan A is . . . . Plan B is . . . . Plan C is . . . ."* These are creative optional agreements that maximize the benefits for all disputants and solve the problem.

Choose the wisest course of action and formalize the agreement with a handshake. *"Let's agree on Plan B!"* A wise agreement is fair to all disputants, maximizes joint benefits, and strengthens disputants' ability to work together cooperatively and resolve future conflicts constructively. It specifies how each disputant should act and how the agreement will be reviewed and renegotiated if it does not work.

Source: Johnson, D.W., and R.T. Johnson. 1991. *Teaching Students To Be Peacemakers.* Edina, MN: Interaction Book Company, pp. 3:52–3:60. Used with permission of the authors and Interaction Book Company.

◊ **Formalizing the agreement.** The mediator formalizes the agreement by completing a report form and having disputants sign it as a commitment to implement the agreement and abide by its conditions.

Faculty Implement the Peacemaker Program

When the students have completed the initial training, the teachers implement the program. Every day the teacher selects two class members to serve as official mediators of any conflicts students cannot resolve themselves. The mediators work in pairs. They wear official T-shirts, patrol the playground and lunchroom, and mediate conflicts. The role of class mediator is rotated throughout the class or school so that all students have an equal chance to serve as class mediator. Teachers and adults who are trained mediators may also mediate student disputes.

Faculty Refine and Upgrade the Students' Skills

Under the TSP program, students receive training every year from the 1st through the 12th grades. Each year, the training becomes more complex and complete, and the faculty teach negotiation and mediation skills weekly throughout the school year to refine and upgrade the students' skills. Students practice the procedures over and over again until they become automatic. Teachers can enhance the TSP program through academic controversy procedures to create intellectual conflicts that increase learning and higher level reasoning and let students practice their conflict resolution skills.

The TSP program is implemented through a combination of bottom-up and top-down strategies. Teams of faculty members are trained to implement the TSP program through 30 to 40 hours of training given throughout the school year or in an intensive summer session. Following the training sessions, trainers provide support to the teaching teams by giving demonstration lessons, helping members prepare lessons, observing their implementation efforts, and providing feedback.

Educators for Social Responsibility

Educators for Social Responsibility (ESR), based in Cambridge, Massachusetts, promotes children's ethical and social development through its programs in conflict resolution, violence prevention, intergroup relations, and character education. ESR helps create peaceable classrooms in schools by providing onsite professional development training with followup support for the schools. By the term "peaceable," ESR means a safe, caring, respectful, and productive learning environment. ESR provides workshops, curriculums, and ongoing support to help educators develop instructional and management practices that foster skill in cooperation, caring communication, appreciation of diversity, expression of feelings, responsible decisionmaking, and conflict resolution.[7]

> Since implementing the Peaceable Classroom approach, I can spend my time doing what I love to do. Teach!
>
> *Kindergarten teacher,*
> *Brookline, Massachusetts*

ESR first conducts a needs assessment of a school or district to help the institution more clearly define the problems it seeks to address, current program strengths, specific needs, and short- and long-term goals. At this stage, ESR recommends the creation of a program steering committee, multiyear planning, voluntary staff participation in training, and the development of local leadership capacity.

> We attended two ESR conflict resolution institutes and brought one of their trainers into our school for 3 days. Since we started this work, so many wonderful things have been happening.
>
> *High school English teacher,*
> *South Bend, Indiana*

ESR Core 4-Day Training Model

The ESR model provides a theoretical background on key topics such as social and emotional learning and developmentally appropriate classroom teaching activities. Woven throughout the training are direct instruction strategies, ideas for incorporating conflict resolution into the curriculum, classroom management ideas, and discipline applications.

This training is participatory and experiential, placing emphasis on community building. Participants in workshops develop action plans appropriate to their classrooms and schools. A major premise is that teachers are taught to model the behavior they seek to teach through direct instruction, and schools develop and reflect the values they seek to nurture among young people in all facets of their program.

ESR recommends that students and teachers make decisions together about classroom norms and guidelines at the beginning of the school year and that teachers provide early instruction in problem solving and decisionmaking so that the skills can be used and reinforced throughout the year.

Ongoing Followup and Support

A staff development specialist provides onsite followup. The activities offered include demonstrations of teaching, coaching, planning, and problem solving. For many teachers, seeing is believing, and the opportunity to watch a staff development specialist model the teaching of conflict resolution for their students is essential. Colleagues who go through the training together are encouraged to meet, share ideas, and discuss difficulties on a periodic basis.

Interviews 6 to 18 months after conflict resolution education training and followup sessions have revealed that participants bring new ways of thinking about teaching and learning to their classrooms. Teachers transform their classrooms, empowering young people to help create a caring classroom community in which they use conflict resolution skills daily. Even more significant change results when a critical mass of teachers engaged in creating and sustaining peaceable classrooms is joined by counselors, administrators, parents, and others to forge a peaceable school and connections to other conflict resolution initiatives in the community.

The ESR peaceable classroom model helps teachers naturally integrate conflict resolution and intergroup relations into their classrooms through direct instruction and reinforcement of skills. It also helps them foster desired behavior through teachable moments and institute systematic classroom management practices.

Notes

1. Kreidler, W. 1990. *Elementary Perspectives I: Teaching Concepts of Peace and Conflict*. Cambridge, MA: Educators for Social Responsibility, p. 43.

2. Johnson, D., and R. Johnson. 1995. *Reducing School Violence Through Conflict Resolution*. Alexandria, VA: Association for Supervisors and Curriculum Development, p. 25.

3. Ibid., pp. 104–105.

4. Ohio Department of Education and Ohio Commission on Dispute Resolution and Conflict Management. 1995. *Conflict Management Resource Guide for Elementary Schools*. Columbus, OH: Ohio Commission on Dispute Resolution and Conflict Management, pp. 7–8.

5. Miller-Lieber, C. 1994. *Making Choices About Conflict, Security, and Peacemaking — Part I: Personal Perspectives*. Cambridge, MA: Educators for Social Responsibility, p. 11.

6. Johnson, D.W., and R.T. Johnson. 1987, 1991, 1995. *Teaching Students To Be Peacemakers*. Edina, MN: Interaction Book Company. For more information, see the section "Peaceable Classroom" in appendix B.

7. Several ESR curriculums are listed under "Peaceable Classroom" in appendix B.

Chapter 5: Peaceable School Approach

Peaceable School: A comprehensive whole-school methodology that builds on the peaceable classroom approach by using conflict resolution as a system of operation for managing the school as well as the classroom. Conflict resolution principles and processes are learned and utilized by every member of the school community—librarians, teachers, counselors, students, principals, and parents.

The peaceable school approach integrates conflict resolution into the operation of the school. Every member of the school community learns and uses conflict resolution concepts and skills. Peaceable school climates reflect caring, honesty, cooperation, and appreciation for diversity. As comprehensive whole-school programs, peaceable schools incorporate:

♦ Cooperative learning environments.

♦ Direct instruction and practice of conflict resolution skills and processes.

♦ Noncoercive school and classroom management systems.

♦ Integration of conflict resolution concepts and skills into the curriculum.

Peaceable school programs challenge youth and adults to believe that a nonviolent, diverse society is a realistic and desirable goal. Peaceable schools value and encourage diversity and promote peacemaking as the normative behavior of adults and students. Participants in the peaceable school apply conflict resolution skills to address interpersonal and intergroup problems and issues that confront students, faculty, administrators, and parents. The objectives of peacemaking are to achieve personal, group, and institutional goals and to maintain cooperative relationships.

In the peaceable school, the pervasive theme touching the interactions between students, between students and adults, and between adults is the value of human dignity and self-esteem.[1]

The Community Board Program (CBP) was one of the first to recognize the value of moving beyond the peer mediation approach to a whole-school approach to conflict resolution education within schools and across school districts. Recognizing that practice in communication and problem-solving skills in the classroom would better prepare students to deal constructively with conflict and to use existing peer mediation programs, CBP developed elementary and secondary classroom curriculums, shifting from an approach that reacts to school conflicts (peer mediation) to one that seeks to prevent them. To change fundamental beliefs about conflict and systems for dealing with conflict, CBP sought to introduce as many school-related personnel as possible to conflict resolution education and to train them in conflict resolution concepts and skills.

The peaceable school approach incorporates the process curriculum, mediation, and peaceable classroom approaches. The peaceable classroom is the unit block of the peaceable school because it is where students gain the knowledge and skills needed to resolve conflicts creatively and where the majority of conflicts are addressed.[2]

The success of conflict resolution in the peaceable school program depends on the school's social climate. Peaceable school programs offer all members of the school community training in the problem-solving processes of conflict resolution. Consensus decisionmaking characterizes each classroom, and negotiation is used by all members of the school community to resolve conflicts equitably. Peer mediation can be applied schoolwide and as a service in the classroom to help disputing students settle their differences constructively. Peaceable school programs incorporate conflict resolution into the school's operations, affecting relationships between all members of the school community, including parents. Effective conflict resolution behavior requires participants to develop mutual appreciation and respect. The successful development of conflict resolution skills depends above all on the absence of coercion.[3]

Peaceable School Transformation

The peaceable school approach supports the school community in addressing specific elements that will transform the school. These elements are not a developmental sequence but entry points to initiating a peaceable school program. The peaceable school emerges in stages, coming to fruition once all transformations have taken place. The elements of transformation include:

♦ Instituting conflict resolution training for adults.

♦ Designing behavior expectations and management systems in concert with conflict resolution theory.

♦ Building cooperation by incorporating cooperative learning and interaction activities into the classroom.

♦ Developing the scope and sequence of conflict resolution skills taught to students.

♦ Providing opportunities for an age-appropriate understanding of conflict—definitions, origins, needs, resources, values, choices for response, consequences of choices, and opportunities— and of peace and peacemaking.

♦ Providing opportunities for an age-appropriate understanding of the principles of conflict resolution based on integrative negotiation theory. These principles include separating people from the problem; focusing on interests, not positions; inventing options for mutual gain; and using fair criteria.

♦ Providing opportunities for each student to learn and practice problem-solving strategies of negotiation and/or consensus decisionmaking within the classroom.

♦ Providing opportunities for students to serve as mediators in their classrooms to help peers resolve issues that they choose not to resolve or cannot resolve through negotiation or consensus decisionmaking.

♦ Providing mediation training for those who want to become mediators in the schoolwide program.

♦ Developing an evaluation process to reach the goal of becoming a peaceable school.

Systemic Change

Typical school academic and disciplinary policies and practices often contradict the peaceful resolution of conflicts. Peaceable schools have reviewed and rethought such operations. Unless the operation of the system corresponds to the desired behavior of the individuals within the system, the contradictory messages will result in confusion and unclear expectations. As David Johnson and Roger Johnson, co-directors of the Conflict Resolution and Cooperative Learning Center of the University of Minnesota, point out:

> It makes no sense to talk of constructive conflict management in schools structured competitively. The first step in teaching students the procedures for managing conflicts, therefore, is creating a cooperative context in which conflicts are defined as mutual problems to be resolved in ways that benefit everyone involved.[4]

In competitive systems, individuals usually focus on short-term self-interests and try to maximize their own goals at the expense of others. In cooperative systems, individuals focus on long-term, mutual interests and try to maximize joint solutions. When cooperation is promoted throughout the school, the problem-solving processes of conflict resolution seem natural, logical, and desirable. Cooperative systems create a context in which conflicts can be resolved constructively and reduce the factors that place individuals at risk for using violence.

Many methods of school behavior management are based on punishment rather than discipline. Such programs gain student compliance through externally imposed behavior expectations that are enforced through coercion. In schools that function in this way, the most significant observable behavior—the adult model—is contrary to conflict resolution principles—respect, tolerance, and appreciation for differences. Gisela Konopka has commented that:

> Obedience is demanded to achieve a person with discipline, but this is a discipline that comes from the outside and works only when one is afraid of someone who is stronger than oneself. We do need discipline, an inner discipline to order our life. What is inner discipline? To my thinking it is the opposite of blind obedience. It is the development of a sense of values.[5]

Table 2 contrasts punishment practices with discipline practices.

The goal of the peaceable school is to create a schoolwide discipline program focused on empowering students to regulate and control their own behavior. The program allows educators to model an orderly, productive system accomplished through cooperation and persistent pursuit of constructive behavior. Students are provided alternative ways to behave, not just told to refrain from behaving in a particular manner. The behavior management program thus becomes an educational program. The problem-solving processes of conflict resolution enable students to achieve principled responses. The following sections present two examples of peaceable school approaches.

Resolving Conflict Creatively Program

The Resolving Conflict Creatively Program (RCCP) is one of the initiatives of Educators for Social Responsibility (ESR—see chapter 4, page 37). In RCCP, adults reach young people by relating

to them daily in their homes, schools, and communities. RCCP requires the support of the highest levels of the school's administration before the program is implemented. A participating school district must make RCCP part of its vision for change and commit to multiyear involvement to ensure proper institutionalization of the program. The RCCP approach involves five components: professional development for teachers and other staff, regular classroom instruction based on a kindergarten through 12th grade (K–12) curriculum, peer mediation, administrator training, and parent training.[6]

> It was a whole different philosophy for me—the way I looked at the world. Children taking responsibility for themselves; that was very different for me. For the first time in my life, I was hearing people say in a school setting: "It's okay to be different." All of a sudden here was a program saying: "You are all good people. You all have something to contribute." I was exposed to a rainbow coalition of children who were learning how to get along. It was just wonderful.
>
> *Teacher, Anchorage, Alaska*

Professional Development for Teachers and Other Staff

A 25-hour introductory course is provided for teachers interested in implementing RCCP in their classrooms. This training presents the theory and methods of conflict resolution, intercultural understanding, and emotional and social literacy; prepares participants to model and teach these skills in their classrooms; illustrates ways to incorporate conflict resolution strategies and skills into academic subjects; and demonstrates creative teaching techniques such as role-playing, interviewing, brainstorming, small-group sharing, and cooperative learning teams.

The staff development component gives teachers the opportunity to receive feedback on lessons that they teach and see skilled practitioners give demonstration lessons in the classroom. They can also plan classroom activities and find resources

Table 2: Punishment Versus Discipline

Punishment	Discipline
Expresses power of an authority; causes pain to the recipient; based on retribution or revenge; concerned with actions in the past.	Based on logical or natural consequences that embody the reality of a social order (rules that one must learn and accept to function productively in society); concerned with actions in the present.
Arbitrary—probably applied inconsistently and unconditionally; does not accept or acknowledge exceptions or mitigating circumstances.	Consistent; accepts that the behaving individual is doing the best he or she can do for now.
Imposed by an authority with responsibility assumed by the one administering the punishment and responsibility avoided by the one receiving the punishment.	Comes from within, with responsibility assumed by the disciplined individual who desires that responsibility; presumes that conscience is internal.
Closes options for the punished individual, who must pay for a behavior that has already occurred.	Opens options for the individual, who can choose new behavior.
As a teaching strategy, usually reinforces a failure identity. Essentially negative and short-term, without sustained personal involvement of either teacher or learner.	As a teaching strategy, is active and involves close, sustained, personal involvement of both teacher and learner; emphasizes the development of more successful behavior.
Characterized by open or concealed anger; easy and expedient; a poor model of expectations.	Friendly and supportive; provides a model of quality behavior.
Focuses on strategies intended to control behavior of learner; rarely results in positive changes in behavior; may increase subversiveness or result in temporary suppression of behavior; at best, produces compliance.	Usually results in a change in behavior that is more successful, acceptable, and responsible; develops the capacity for self-evaluation of behavior.

Source: Crawford, D., R. Bodine, and R. Hoglund. 1993. *The School for Quality Learning.* Champaign, IL: Research Press, Inc., p. 187. Reprinted with permission of the authors and Research Press.

in collaboration with an RCCP consultant. RCCP staff developers visit newly trained teachers 6 to 10 times during their first year and varying numbers of times in subsequent years. The staff developer conducts bimonthly followup meetings after school so that teachers can receive additional training, share their experiences and concerns, problem-solve, and plan schoolwide events.

K–12 Curriculum

Teachers use the K–12 curriculum to demonstrate that there are other ways to deal with conflict than passivity or aggression, to develop skills to make those choices in real-life situations, to increase understanding and appreciation of different cultures, and to empower youth to play a significant role in creating a more peaceful world.

I've seen changes in some of the kids at school since we started this program. They look at things differently now. They don't act the same; they try to be more peaceful now. I think we are really changing the gangs on this campus. There used to be a lot of gangs before, writing in the bathrooms and all that, but it's sort of stopped. It's more peaceful now.

Ninth grade student, Vista, California

RCCP developed the curriculum in collaboration with participating teachers. It provides effective teaching strategies on the elementary, middle, and high school levels. Curriculum themes include peace and conflict, communication, affirmation, fostering cooperation, working with feelings, negotiation and mediation, appreciating diversity, bias awareness, countering bias, peacemakers, and envisioning a positive future. Some individual skills integrated into these themes include active listening, perspective taking, dealing with anger, assertiveness, win-win negotiation, understanding cultures, and avoiding expressions of bias.

RCCP encourages teachers to set aside 30 to 45 minutes at least once a week throughout the school year for a specific workshop in conflict resolution prepared from the curriculum guide. Teachers also integrate conflict resolution lessons, strategies, and skills into the regular academic program.

Peer Mediation

The school must implement the RCCP curriculum for at least a year before beginning peer mediation. Peer mediation reinforces the emerging problem-solving skills students learn through the curriculum. The students and teachers select a cadre of students representative of the school's diverse cultures and backgrounds to be peer mediators. Once trained, elementary students take turns being "on duty" on the playground during recess. Wearing special mediator T-shirts and working in teams with their adult advisors nearby, they help students talk out their disputes. Middle school and high school peer

mediators do not work on the playground but listen to disputes in a room designated for mediation.

Administrator Training

Training is provided for administrators to introduce the concepts of conflict resolution and bias awareness and encourage them to embrace and model the humane and creative approaches to dealing with conflict that teachers are implementing through the classroom curriculum.

Parent Training

Parents participate in a 12-hour training in the skills and concepts of conflict resolution and intergroup relations so they can make their homes more peaceful and help their children become adept at using the conflict resolution skills learned at school. As they learn ways of dealing with conflict and prejudice at home, they become more effective leaders in their schools and communities. Parents may become trainers of other parents by participating in a district-level 60-hour training program.

The primary impetus for starting the program in my school was to reduce violence, but it goes beyond that because there is a strong preventive measure. By teaching conflict resolution skills, we're creating an environment that says it's OK to have anger and conflict, which are a natural part of life. We're saying that you can have these emotions and these conflicts and not have violence, which our culture glamorizes.

Principal, Brooklyn, New York

Illinois Institute for Dispute Resolution

The Creating the Peaceable School (CPS) program of the Illinois Institute for Dispute Resolution (IIDR—see also chapter 3, page 27) focuses on applying conflict resolution principles to school and classroom management in order to encourage enduring systemic changes vital to the success of a peaceable school approach.[7] The CPS program may be implemented within a school or school district. IIDR helps schools and school districts develop a comprehensive plan for program development based on their identified needs and resources.

> I have a habit of finishing sentences for my older daughter. While she talks, I sit there nodding impatiently and then I finish her thought for her. After the workshop last weekend, I decided to try to stop doing that. It wasn't long before she put me to the test. But this time, I was patient. I gave her my attention. I didn't interrupt her. And when she was done, I actually paraphrased what I heard her saying. She was shocked. She just stood there. I could see tears in her eyes. "Mommy," she said, "you really listened to me."
>
> *Parent, New York City*

Fundamental Skill Areas

Six skills are fundamental to the achievement of a peaceable school: building a peaceable climate, understanding conflict, understanding peace and peacemaking, mediation, negotiation, and group problem solving. The IIDR curriculum provides the educator with a theoretical overview of the skill area and then gives a number of activities and strategies to engage students in developing a knowledge base and in acquiring these skills. Each activity contains step-by-step procedures to be followed with the students and can be used in a class workshop, team project, learning center, cooperative learning situation, or class meeting. The skill areas are described below.

Building a Peaceable Climate. Responsibility and cooperation are the foundation for all other skills in the peaceable school. To manage student behavior without coercion, adults must take the perspective that effective behavior is the responsibility of the student and strive to develop a sense of responsibility in each. Students then begin to make responsible choices guided by their rights and corresponding responsibilities.

Understanding Conflict. For students to engage in successful conflict resolution, they must have a shared understanding of the nature of conflict. The program provides information and activities that instill a shared understanding of the nature and causes of conflict, the possible responses to conflict, and its potential benefits. The idea that psychological needs are the underlying cause of conflict is useful to students as they seek to resolve disputes through common interests.

Understanding Peace and Peacemaking. Students are taught to observe peacemaking and peacebreaking behaviors within the school and classroom. Peacemaking activities help students understand and practice the concept of peace. Students learn that specific behaviors are associated with peacemaking, namely, appreciating diversity, understanding perceptions, empathizing, dealing with emotions, managing anger, countering bias, and communicating. The principles of conflict resolution are also taught as peacemaking behaviors.

Mediation. Mediation is defined as assisted conflict resolution between disputants for use within the classroom and as a schoolwide vehicle for resolving conflicts. Training activities cover a mediation process that allows students to gain the skills to act as neutral third parties when facilitating conflict resolution between disputants.

> When you talk it out, like when you can sit down and talk about it, you're not as mad. That's the way I see it. When you start talkin' about it, the anger just dies down. You just become more civilized; you go back into your regular state of mind.
>
> *Student, Alternative High School, Baltimore, Maryland*

Negotiation. Disputants learn to resolve their conflicts unassisted by stating their individual needs, focusing on their interests rather than their positions, and generating options for mutual gain.

Group Problem Solving. Group problem solving is taught as a creative strategy for dealing with conflicts that involve a number of students within the classroom, within groups, and between groups in the school. The group's responsibility is to achieve a consensus decision that, when implemented, will resolve the conflict.

> The conflict resolution training provided our staff with skills and processes for real and effective collaboration. I do not think we have ever worked together so well. We are able to make decisions that address our goals and interests without feeling threatened or angered by change. We are reaching consensus and making new commitments.
>
> *Principal, Chicago, Illinois*

Other Areas of Development

The CPS program includes three additional areas of outreach: (1) intensive professional development (training, coaching, and technical assistance for administrators, teachers, and support staff), (2) parent education, and (3) community initiatives.

Professional Development. IIDR approaches professional development as an opportunity to create a learning community among teachers, administrators, and support staff in which members help and support each other. Part of this process includes examining their handling of conflict in their private and public lives, particularly in their relationships with students.

The CPS program emphasizes the need for introductory workshops with followup strategic planning and technical support. IIDR consultants provide onsite followup in schools to support school staff—teachers, administrators, and support personnel—as the peaceable school program is being implemented. Professional development includes a range of activities such as demonstrating teaching methods in

classrooms, helping teachers plan, observing classes, providing feedback, and coaching.

Parent Education. The peaceable school is brought to parents through Peaceable Home workshops, which are given at locations such as public, private, and alternative schools; public housing projects; and community centers. These workshops teach parents the skills and concepts of conflict resolution. Parents learn to apply these concepts in their homes, schools, and communities.

Community Initiatives. In creating peaceable schools, school administrators and teachers play a critical role in reaching out to leaders and families in the community to engage them in conflict resolution strategies. The peaceable school expands into the peaceable neighborhood through extension to parents, police, churches, and neighborhood coalitions. The following IIDR youth and community activities mobilize youth, parents, community activists, agencies, and organizations to help create peaceable schools and neighborhoods:

◆ **Peer education.** High school youth are recruited to form a Youth Peace Corps trained to teach conflict resolution strategies, including anger management, to their peers and to middle and elementary school students. This group must represent a cross section of the entire student body. These highly trained youth provide strong role models for younger students because they teach these skills in the school and use their skills in the neighborhood.

> I was so impressed with how seriously the kids took the training and how well they did. They were very much taken by the whole notion of conflict resolution. We adults that assisted with training got caught up in the simulations and resorted to our "old ways." The students seemed able to see the problems much more simply. It was not difficult for them at all.
>
> *Parent, Wilmette, Illinois*

◆ **Community training.** Positive youth development is supported by the establishment of partnerships with youth-serving organizations and those who encounter youth in conflict. Conflict resolution training may be provided for police departments, park districts, Boys & Girls Clubs, the Urban League, and other interested agencies and organizations that work with youth. The program recruits specific personnel from these agencies and organizations to attend community training.

◆ **Police-youth-community dialogs.** Afterschool sessions on site and Saturday retreats in the country bring youth, police, and community members together to learn about one another and practice conflict resolution skills. In working sessions, participants play a series of team games designed to demonstrate how teams can solve problems together. These activities lead to a common vision and allow participants to confront their differences as well as their interdependency.

Through its CPS program, IIDR builds a shared vision that is a foundation for change among all members of the school community. The curriculum guides schools toward a systemic transformation. Schools build the capacity to manage conflict and change as they develop and implement a peaceable school program.

Notes

1. Bodine, R., D. Crawford, and F. Schrumpf. 1994. *Creating the Peaceable School: A Comprehensive Program for Teaching Conflict Resolution.* Champaign, IL: Research Press, Inc., p. 2.

2. Ibid, p. 3.

3. Ibid, p. 29.

4. Johnson, D., and R. Johnson. 1993. "Cooperative Learning and Conflict Resolution." *The Fourth R* 42:8.

5. Konopka, G. 1985. "A Renewed Look at Human Development, Human Needs, and Human Services." *Proceedings of the Annual Gisela Konopka Lectureship.* St. Paul, MN: University of Minnesota Center for Youth Development and Research, p. 186.

6. The RCCP curriculums include *Resolving Conflict Creatively: A Teaching Guide for Grades Kindergarten Through Six,* 1993, and *Resolving Conflict Creatively: A Teaching Guide for Secondary Schools,* 1990. New York, NY: RCCP National Center. For more information, see "Peaceable School" in appendix B.

7. Bodine et al., *Creating the Peaceable School,* 1994. For more information, see "Peaceable School," appendix B.

Chapter 6: Juvenile Justice and Alternative Education Initiatives

For juvenile justice facilities and alternative schools, implementing conflict resolution means changing the institution's approach to internal conflicts from a punitive one to one that uses problem-solving methods. In these settings, conflict resolution programs are introduced to supplement, not replace, existing disciplinary policies and procedures. Given opportunities for positive expression and problem resolution, youth learn alternatives to violent and self-defeating behavior.

Conflict resolution programs for juvenile justice facilities and for alternative schools serving delinquent and at-risk youth address similar issues. These youth tend to demonstrate self-destructive, antisocial, or violent behavior to a greater degree than even the more behaviorally challenged youth in regular schools. In both cases, an effective conflict resolution program must address the psychological needs and the developmental stage of the youth.

The impediments to behavioral self-awareness in delinquent and at-risk youth are considerable and pervasive. Typically, their ability to evaluate their own behavior is underdeveloped, and they are seriously deficient in the foundation abilities of conflict resolution, especially orientation, perception, and emotional abilities. Many have an ingrained sense of failure and view success as beyond their reach and ability.

These problems often go beyond the purview of conflict resolution programs, which do not offer therapy. However, young people who need therapy can still participate in and profit from conflict resolution programs. At issue is whether the behavioral challenges faced by these youth can be addressed while they are receiving conflict resolution education or whether their problems require initial

> Peacemaking is not easy. In many ways, it is much more difficult than making war. But its great rewards cannot be measured in ordinary terms.
>
> *Former President Jimmy Carter[1]*

attention. A benefit of conflict resolution education is the development of the youth's ability to apply the training in appropriate situations. The extent of therapy needed will be determined by how well the youth applies the conflict resolution training. The greater the gap between the youth's standard behavior and the desired behavior of conflict resolution, the greater the demand for practice and coaching.

Juvenile Justice Facilities

The juvenile justice correctional facility provides opportunities over alternative education settings, because the students live and attend school within the facility. Programs taught in these facilities allow more time for training and practice in conflict resolution.

Many juvenile offenders have deficits in cognitive skills. They tend to be undersocialized and lack the values, attitudes, reasoning abilities, and social skills required for positive social interaction. These individuals have not acquired the skills and strategies for constructive relationship building and problem solving, nor have they bonded with anyone who exhibits these behaviors. By teaching the foundation abilities and problem-solving processes of conflict resolution (see chapter 1), the juvenile justice facility can facilitate the development of social competency in these youth, so that they no longer alienate themselves from mainstream culture. The following section describes a conflict resolution program in a juvenile justice setting in California.

The Community Board Program

In 1987, with support from California's Office of Criminal Justice Planning, the Community Board Program began to explore how the Conflict Manager (peer mediation) program might be implemented in juvenile treatment facilities, known in some jurisdictions as "ranches." In California and other States, these county-operated facilities are the last opportunity for the rehabilitation of serious and violent juvenile offenders before they enter the Youth Authority, the juvenile equivalent of the adult prison system.

Over time, unresolved conflicts can affect the entire facility. They consume the time and energy of counselors, extend the sentences of wards, lower the morale of counselors and wards, and make the atmosphere tense and anxious. The Conflict Manager program helps everyone involved deal with conflict more effectively.

> Our wards are here in part because they have experienced conflict in their lives and did not know how to resolve it appropriately. The Conflict Manager program teaches these young men the skills to approach a conflict in a mature manner and resolve it in a socially acceptable fashion.
>
> *Superintendent, Harold Holden Ranch for Boys, Morgan Hill, California*

The heart of a Conflict Manager program is a face-to-face meeting between the disputants in which they talk about their problems with the help of conflict managers, who are wards of these facilities selected and trained to serve as mediators for their peers. Throughout the conflict management process, the disputants are required to take responsibility for the problem and its solution. The conflict manager's responsibility is to help the disputants communicate more effectively and understand one another's point of view. The disputants then come to their own agreement, one they are more likely to keep. The objectives of conflict management are to rebuild or establish a positive relationship between the disputants and gradually spread the belief in and use of peaceful and constructive conflict resolution skills throughout the facility.[2]

Voluntary Participation

Participation in the program is voluntary. Wards may be referred by a counselor to see the conflict managers, but once there, they have the choice not to participate, with no penalty for their decision. Wards have this choice because conflict management requires the active participation of both disputants. If both are committed to finding a resolution to their problem, both will work hard to express their points of view and listen to each other. This is impossible if one party does not want to participate.

Because conflict management is voluntary, it is never a replacement for disciplinary action. If wards are offered conflict management as an alternative to punishment, their motives for participating may be clouded and the process ineffective. The goal is to provide early intervention for peaceful problem solving before rules are broken or conflicts escalate. When wards break facility rules, staff take the usual disciplinary steps. Afterward, they can suggest meeting with conflict managers to express and resolve core issues and avoid further conflict. In this way, the Conflict Manager program supplements rather than replaces the regular disciplinary system.

Types of Disputes Handled by Conflict Managers

Conflict managers are equipped to handle many of the day-to-day disputes that arise in a juvenile facility setting, such as name calling, serious "horseplay," and conflicts over things in short supply—time at the pool table or in the weight room, a chance to watch a favorite television program, the attention of a popular counselor, or access to supplies such as toiletries.

Low self-esteem, which is common among youth in juvenile facilities, is often the source of these conflicts. For many of these youth, bullying or "putting down" someone is the only means of achieving status among peers. As a counselor in a juvenile facility remarked, "These kids don't know how to walk away from a fight without losing face."

> Virtually all of our young men are gang affiliated and come from families where conflict was resolved through abuse or violence. . . . Conflict management goes beyond stabilizing the institution; it gives the youth a chance to take on a positive role, learn verbal skills, and overcome violent tendencies. It not only benefits the kids, but also the community to which they will return.
>
> *Juvenile facility director, Camp Miller,*
> *Los Angeles County*

Types of Conflicts Not Handled

Conflict managers are not asked to intervene in a violent confrontation, especially when weapons are involved. After the heat of the battle has passed, the disputants may meet with conflict managers to find ways to avoid further violence.

Other matters typically excluded from conflict manager attention are disputes between staff and wards. Handling such conflicts may raise staff objections and other programmatic challenges, especially in the case of new programs. However, because some high school mediation programs have successfully handled teacher-student conflicts, it may be possible for juvenile facility programs to expand into this area.

Conflict Manager Selection

Conflict managers are selected jointly by staff and wards to ensure they will have the respect and support of both groups. Generally, the members of each group are asked to make nominations. Staff then review the list of wards who have received the greatest number of nominations and select 12 to 15 out of

this group to enter training. The wards who become conflict managers are seen as leaders by their peers, but frequently "negative" leaders are nominated by their peers and approved by staff. This is done because experience as a conflict manager often draws out the talent of negative leaders, allowing them to make a positive contribution to the facility.

Conflict Manager Training

Because of ward turnover, training for new conflict managers is conducted every few months. Often current conflict managers are asked to assist in training those who are new. Ongoing meetings among conflict managers are held to provide further training, assessment of the program, and group discussions.

During their training, conflict managers learn basic communication skills, such as helping disputants feel comfortable in talking, listening in a way that will defuse anger, and speaking to disputants in a direct but diplomatic way. They also learn about the three-stage conflict management process—the goals of each stage, the questions to ask at each stage, and methods of handling common problems.

Conflict Manager Supervision

Because training in this model should be considered an ongoing process, staff coordinators for the Conflict Manager program meet with the managers for at least 1 hour every week so that they can share their experiences and talk about problems they have encountered in their work. If time allows, conflict managers are asked to role-play a difficult case and discuss it together.

Potential Benefits of Conflict Manager Programs

Conflict Manager programs reduce tensions and save staff time by taking care of conflicts that would otherwise absorb hours of their day. At the same time, wards who participate in conflict management sessions are positively affected because they have the opportunity to experience new ways of dealing with conflict. Also, by resolving conflict constructively before it escalates or requires a counselor, wards can avoid consequences that could lengthen their stay at the facility. The program has a significant impact on conflict managers, helping them to increase their self-esteem, learn to resolve conflicts peacefully, and improve academic achievement.

Working with facilities in three Bay Area counties of California, the Community Board conducted extensive staff development work that included building and training a Site Leadership Team, developing online counselors as conflict manager trainers, and developing a program plan based on the facilities' needs and staff input. Within a period of 9 months to a year, the Community Board staff trained at least 3 groups of 15 young men as conflict managers at each facility, leaving each with a solid, well-prepared team of trainers to continue periodic training of new conflict managers.

> Learning mediation has helped me to realize that there are other methods of solving your problems other than violence. It has also helped me to deal with different types of people.
>
> *16-year-old resident,*
> *Youth Diagnostic and Development Center*

After 3 years, Conflict Manager programs in juvenile facilities are ongoing, and trained youth are helping to resolve disputes for their peers every day. Peer mediation programs have reduced the number and seriousness of conflicts and rule infractions and have limited staff time spent on discipline.

A survey completed at the end of their training asked conflict managers where they thought they might be able to use their new skills other than participating in the Conflict Manager program. Nearly every ward wrote that the skills would be useful in other settings—with family, at a job, or with neighborhood friends. At Holden Ranch, a conflict manager who graduated from the facility called a counselor several months later to say that conflict

resolution skills had helped him change his difficult relationship with his mother.

Studies of recidivism have found that wards are less likely to return to the correctional system if they have steady employment. Other studies show that graduates of juvenile facilities often lose jobs not because they lack technical skills, but because they are unable to resolve problems with co-workers, supervisors, or employers. Thus, it is likely that conflict managers will stay out of the correctional system after they leave the facility. This may be the most important long-term impact of the conflict manager training program.

Alternative Schools

Students in most alternative schools do not differ substantially from students in other schools when it comes to conflict and do not need to be treated differently when developing and implementing a conflict resolution program. Some alternative schools enroll youth with behavioral/emotional disorders, including students who have dropped out or are at risk of dropping out. Many of these youth are involved in the court system and may be in an alternative school because of court dictates. Some are teen parents; some are homeless; others are involved in substance abuse. Although many of these students are intellectually capable, they have often failed academically.

These alternative schools offer a place for students who have demonstrated, in one or many ways, that their behavior is unacceptable in a regular school. Often the participants in these alternative schools have demonstrated the potential for self-destructive, antisocial, or violent behavior. Most students placed in such alternative schools need conflict resolution education because they have experienced numerous conflicts involving other youth, school staff members, and school expectations or rules. They are often in these alternative schools because they escalated rather than deescalated a dispute. These students are clearly prime candidates for conflict resolution education. The following section describes a conflict resolution program in an alternative school in New York.

International Center for Cooperation and Conflict Resolution

The International Center for Cooperation and Conflict Resolution (ICCCR) at Columbia University initiated a conflict resolution project at an alternative high school (AHS) in New York City.[3] The goal of the project was to determine the effects of cooperative learning and conflict resolution training on AHS students.

This AHS was established in 1971 as part of a network of alternative high schools in New York City. It has approximately 180 students and 14 teachers, including a site coordinator, at each of its 4 campuses. Anyone under the age of 19 living anywhere in New York City may apply to any campus of the school. Students may be admitted to the AHS in several ways. Students who have already dropped out or are at risk of dropping out of another school may apply voluntarily, while others are referred by high school counselors or the court system.

Applicants have a broad range of academic skills and poor attendance records. The demographic portrait of the AHS student population at the beginning of the project was striking. The racial composition was 56.9 percent African American, 40.5 percent Hispanic, 2.2 percent white, 0.4 percent Asian, and 0.1 percent Native American; 5.1 percent of the students had limited proficiency in English. There were equal numbers of female and male students, and the average age was 17 years. One-third of the female students were teen parents. The majority of the students came from disadvantaged households, and increasing numbers came from families with risk factors such as drug abuse and homelessness. The achievement rate was well below that of other New York City high schools: the average number of previously acquired high school credits was 20, and dropouts had been out of school for periods ranging from 6 months to 7 years.

Training Components

Initial training of the administrators, coordinators, teachers, and paraprofessionals took place in August 1988; almost all who were eligible participated in the training. The training usually involves afterschool training workshops with the trainer on campus for individual staff development.

ICCCR used the training model for cooperative learning developed by David Johnson and Roger Johnson of the Cooperative Learning Center at the University of Minnesota. Five key elements are involved in cooperative learning.[4] The most important is positive interdependence, meaning that students must perceive that it is to their advantage if other students learn well and to their disadvantage if others do poorly. This can be achieved through mutual goals (goal interdependence), division of labor (task interdependence), and joint rewards (reward interdependence).

In addition, cooperative learning requires face-to-face interaction among students in which they express their positive interdependence. This method also requires individual accountability; that is, each member of the cooperative learning situation is responsible to the others for mastering the material, analyzing the group's performance, and making suggestions for improving cooperation.

ICCCR's conflict resolution training draws upon several sources: Deutsch's theoretical model, which articulates a number of basic principles of conflict resolution training;[5] Raider's training model, which has been widely used by conflict resolution training managers and teachers;[6] Prothrow-Stith's curriculum on violence prevention;[7] and the Community Board Program's curriculums for conflict resolution and mediation.[8] Conflict resolution training is implemented in a variety of ways, depending on the context in which it is to be employed — orientation sessions for new students, family groups, or vocational classes, for example. Role-playing, group activities, and discussion groups are used to apply negotiation skills to the students' lives in home, school, and work settings.

Impact of the ICCCR Conflict Resolution Project

ICCCR results indicate that the positive effects on students trained in conflict resolution and cooperative learning include improved conflict management, social support, and fewer feelings of victimization. As their relations with others improved, these youth experienced increased self-esteem, decreased feelings of anxiety and depression, and more frequent positive feelings of well-being. Greater self-esteem produced a greater sense of control over their fate, which in turn led to higher academic performance. Indirect evidence indicated that the students' work readiness and performance also improved.

The ICCCR project was initiated with the strong support of the principal and assistant principal and the voluntary cooperation of the staff. The conflict resolution training combined resources from a number of curriculums to address the needs of the student population. This project was successfully conducted under considerably more problematic conditions than those most schools experience. The students at this AHS are significantly at risk and face more difficult life circumstances, and their teachers work in an extremely challenging environment, such as within older buildings equipped with fewer resources. The positive results produced by the training under these conditions indicate the significance of administrative support, voluntary cooperation, and relevant learning experiences. These results also suggest that cooperative learning and conflict resolution training are valuable in a wide range of settings.

Notes

1. Carter, J. 1993. *Talking Peace: A Vision for the Next Generation.* New York, NY: Dutton Children's Books, p. xiv.

2. See Holmberg, M., and J. Halligan. 1992. *Conflict Management for Juvenile Treatment Facilities: A Manual for Training and Program Implementation.* San Francisco, CA: Community Board Program, Inc.

3. Deutsch, M., V. Mitchell, Q. Zhang, N. Khattri, L. Tepavac, E.A. Weitzman, and R. Lynch. 1992. *The Effects of Training in Cooperative Learning and Conflict Resolution in an Alternative High School.* New York, NY: Columbia University.

4. Johnson, D., R. Johnson, and E. Holubec. 1986. *Circles of Learning: Cooperation in the Classroom.* Edina, MN: Interaction Book Company.

5. Deutsch, M. 1991 (August). "Educating for a Peaceful World." Presidential address to the Division of Peace Psychology, presented at the Annual Meeting of the American Psychological Association, San Francisco, CA.

6. Raider, E. 1987. *Conflict Resolution.* New Paltz, NY: Ellen Raider International, Inc.

7. Prothrow-Stith, D. 1987. *Violence Prevention: Curriculum for Adolescents.* Newton, MA: Education Development Center.

8. Sadalla, G., M. Henriquez, and M. Holmberg. 1987. *Conflict Resolution: A Secondary Curriculum.* San Francisco, CA: Community Board Program, Inc.

Chapter 7: Parent and Community Initiatives

The impact of school-based conflict resolution programs increases when they are linked with community and parent education programs that allow students to apply their skills in productive ways in a variety of settings. This linkage is important because young people face a challenge in applying conflict resolution training in the community and in the home, especially with others who are not similarly trained.

Parent Education

Children must possess a secure and positive sense of their own identity and their place in the world, and they must acquire character and skills that enable them to live in harmony with their families and the larger community. Development of these skills depends upon trusting and loving relationships, the first and most fundamental of which is between children and their parents. Families are the settings where children's basic needs are met and where they learn lessons about personal relationships and problem solving. For children, families are the basic training ground for developing the capacity to function responsibly and to solve problems peacefully. Educating parents in conflict resolution is essential.

According to Brendtro and Long, any comprehensive effort to eliminate disputes and violence will require a full range of services, including, but not limited to, school-based programs.[2] If patterns of conflict and aggression are to be reversed, primary prevention and early intervention must be priorities.

Primary Prevention

Troubled behavior, once launched, perpetuates itself throughout a person's life. Therefore, interventions

> The circle is a sacred symbol of life. . . . Individual parts within the circle connect with every other; and what happens to one, or what one part does, affects all within the circle.
>
> *Virginia Driving Hawk Sneve*[1]

that affect the lives of young children in families and schools deserve the highest priority. These interventions include:[3]

- **Strengthening parenting bonds.** Children are less prone to violence when their basic needs are met and they are reared in consistent, safe, and loving environments.

- **Teaching children self-discipline.** Beginning in elementary school, all children should be given "basic training" in self-discipline. Teachers can be trained to use naturally occurring discipline problems to create school cultures of nonviolence.

- **Teaching conflict resolution.** Students need to be competent in resolving both conflicts with peers and authority problems with adults. This competence forms the basis for lifelong survival skills.

Early Intervention

It is important to recognize that some youth are at risk for violence in their early years and should be provided with effective, comprehensive experiences in school, at home, and in the community. The following research-validated interventions should be part of a logical system for reducing delinquent and self-defeating behavior:[4]

- **Mentoring at-risk youth.** Every child needs at least one adult who provides unconditional love. Many children suffer from attention deprivation. When parents are unable or unavailable to provide the consistent nurturing and support that children need, mentors can have a profound impact in fulfilling that role.

- **Mentoring and training parents.** Since much early antisocial behavior is caused by inconsistent and harsh discipline, parent training curriculums are important tools for breaking cycles of coercion (abuse and/or violence) and instilling positive parent-child interactions.

- **Targeting bullies.** Peer harassment is an early indicator of lifelong antisocial problems. Without intervention, childhood bullies often develop into violent adults.

Educating parents in conflict resolution is a natural way to bring children's experiences at home and at school closer together. Helping families deal constructively with the inevitable conflicts of family living allows parents to disengage from inconsistent and harsh, punitive behaviors. When parents model effective behaviors in conflict situations, they present powerful teaching examples to children. In their book, *Battles, Hassles, Tantrums & Tears*, Beekman and Holmes offer parents strategies for coping with conflict and making peace at home.[5] Their program, C.H.O.I.C.E.S. for Managing Conflict, offers guidelines for adult responses to conflict (see figure 5).

Although vital to early childhood education, parent initiatives are a potential link between schools and homes, regardless of the age of the youth involved. The more youth experience constructive approaches to conflict, especially at school or at home, the more likely they will internalize these behaviors.

Parents as Teachers Program. Most early childhood education programs include parent involvement and parent education components for intervening in behaviors that promote a cycle of violence. The Parents as Teachers program, which originated in St. Louis, Missouri, is based on the idea that early childhood experiences are critical in laying the foundation for success in school and life, and that parents are children's first and most influential teachers.

Parents as Teachers is a home-school-community partnership designed to provide parents with information and support in the development of prosocial skills. The goal is to help parents prepare their children for success in school and life throughout the critical years from birth to entry into kindergarten. Through personal home visits by child development professionals, group meetings with other parents, and play groups for parents and children together, parents are given alternatives to corporal punishment along with developmental information that promotes realistic expectations for their children's behavior. This program provides a foundation of sharing, empathy, and accountability in young children that prepares them for conflict resolution education when they are older.

Parents Anonymous, Inc. Recognizing the link between child abuse and juvenile delinquency, the Office of Juvenile Justice and Delinquency Prevention (OJJDP) began to support Parents Anonymous, Inc. (PA), in 1994. Because minority children are overrepresented in the juvenile justice system, this collaborative effort between OJJDP and PA focuses on bringing PA's comprehensive model of neighborhood-based, shared leadership to families in low-income, high-crime areas. This national initiative is being implemented in 11 States by PA organizations dedicated to serving a range of ethnic groups, including Native Americans, African Americans, Asians, Latinos, and Appalachians.

Conflict resolution is one of the elements of PA's multifaceted program. Parents are given the opportunity to observe, practice, and learn conflict resolution skills and problem-solving processes. These skills and processes are taught in the context of family life, the worksite, and personal friendships. They are practiced in weekly group sessions as conflicts occur.

Franklin Mediation Services and Head Start of Franklin County, Massachusetts. These two agencies joined to create a project providing comprehensive direct services in the form of mediation, parent and staff mediation training, and bias awareness training. Parents of Head Start pupils, Head Start staff, and community residents attend workshops to learn conflict resolution techniques. In addition, Head Start clients receive direct mediation services

Figure 5: C.H.O.I.C.E.S. for Managing Conflict

- **C ommand:** Give clear directions and specifically state what you want the child to do in a non-humiliating manner—"Clean up your room before visiting your friend."

- **H umor or surprise:** Use nonsarcastic humor or do the unexpected to defuse an explosive situation. For example, channel kids who are bickering over a toy into a different activity—"Let's pretend we're robots and clean up the family room."

- **O ffer choices:** Give a choice between two options—"You can _____ or _____," or "When you _____, then you can _____."

- **I gnore:** Choose not to address the conflict or unacceptable behavior by withholding attention.

- **C ompromise:** Seek a middle ground by finding a solution that partially satisfies both parties—"If you ____, then I'll ____."

- **E ncourage problem solving:** Work together to explore the disagreement, generate alternatives, and find a solution that satisfies the needs of both parties—"What can we do to meet everyone's needs?"

- **S tructure the environment:** Rearrange people, room structure, or objects to reduce conflict. For example, separate kids who are fighting in the car by moving them to different seats.

Source: Beekman, S., and J. Holmes. 1993. *Battles, Hassles, Tantrums & Tears: Strategies for Coping with Conflict and Making Peace at Home.* New York, NY: Hearst Books, William Morrow & Company, Inc., Publishers, p. 90. Reprinted with permission of the authors and William Morrow & Company, Inc.

that help resolve conflicts between children and parents, couples, and tenants and landlords. Program staff also developed a mediation curriculum for use in Head Start classrooms. Advocates who regularly work with Head Start families report that the concepts and skills learned in the program become part of family conflict management. The consistent use of negotiation skills helps families resolve problems without third-party intervention and without violence.

Community Programs

Some youth-centered conflict resolution programs have originated in the community rather than in schools. Both community-to-school and school-to-community programs make critical linkages that enhance the quality of life in each arena. Community programs provide a common conflict resolution vocabulary. The focus of many of these programs is to provide youth with conflict resolution training through youth clubs, churches, court referral services, and other youth-service organizations, and to reinforce the lessons learned through followup training at school.

The advantages of community-based conflict resolution programs linked with a school program are access to common trainers and volunteers such as youth, parents, and teachers; increased cooperation between schools and communities; and an institutional base for long-term conflict resolution training in a given area. Additionally, community-to-school cooperation provides an ongoing laboratory for refining conflict resolution theory and for finding a balance between theory and practice that encourages youth to apply their training in the local living environment. Profiles of a variety of community-based programs are presented in the following sections.

Community Mediation Programs

Community mediation centers, located in more than 600 communities in the United States, have initiated the community-to-school link in developing and implementing conflict resolution programs for children, youth, and families. These centers, which are typically nonprofit, community-based agencies, use trained community volunteers to provide a wide range of mediation services to youth and adults. The majority of these centers have initiated mediation and conflict resolution programs for youth in schools and other settings. Mediation centers have pioneered applications of mediation for youth and families, including truancy, parent/child, gang, and suspension mediation, as well as applications in juvenile correctional settings. In addition, centers have collaborated with other youth-serving agencies and schools in the development of prevention and intervention strategies and initiatives to prevent youth violence.

Community mediation centers provide an institutional base for long-term conflict resolution training in the communities in which they are located. When conflicts flow from the school to the community and from the community to the school, the mediation center provides the appropriate links and continuum of services. The National Association for Community Mediation, listed in appendix A, can provide information about local services.

Lawyers Adopt-a-School Program

The Lawyers Adopt-a-School Program of the American Bar Association, Section of Dispute Resolution, encourages the establishment of mediation programs in elementary, middle, and high schools. A law firm becomes a sponsor of a school peer mediation program by helping to provide training and financial and moral support. The law firm works with the school to develop and maintain a school mediation program, to provide resources for the initial training of the mediators and for continued support of the program, to enrich the school by involving the community and the business sector, to provide role models, and to assist teachers in developing ways to expand the curriculum. The school and the law firm enter into an agreement that identifies the aims of the partnership, the activities each partner will undertake, the resources to be provided, and the length of time the partnership will last. After an agreement is reached, the mutual relationship is ongoing for the duration of the school year.

East Cleveland Youth Services Mobile Mediation Project

One of the purposes of this project is to address the afterschool conflicts that tend to boil over into violence on East Cleveland's inner-city streets. Project staff (parents, youth, teachers, and principals) who travel the neighborhood in a mobile home are highly visible and offer alternatives for settling fights between volatile groups of youth. Staff are trained to recognize signs of imminent conflict and to apply the skills of mediation. The mobility of the project makes mediation more accessible. Mediation is conducted in the mobile home, and sometimes the disputing parties are taken to the community mediation center. The East Cleveland Youth Mediation Services program estimates that the mobile mediation project serves between 2,000 and 3,000 people a year by conducting community and school conflict resolution education workshops and mediations.

Roxbury Conflict Resolution Project

The Conflict Management Group (CMG), the Unitarian Universalist Urban Ministry (UUUM), the First Church Program of Boston, and the Program for Young Negotiators (PYN) are partners in the Roxbury Conflict Resolution Project in Massachusetts. This community-based conflict resolution training program has three primary goals:

♦ Joining with community youth in working from the ground up to develop new ways of understanding conflict, its causes, and its consequences.

♦ Assisting youth to learn effective skills and techniques to deal proactively with conflict.

♦ Teaching conflict resolution skills to youth and developing a corps of qualified peer trainers to transfer their learning through a comprehensive community outreach program.

Community Component. Conflict resolution programs for youth provide a range of functions and meet both educational and environmental needs. An important aspect of the environmental function is to seek out youth and give them a voice in developing such a program. CMG and UUUM have devoted significant time and resources to giving youth a voice in designing this program. The project is deeply committed to the idea that when young people have a role in building a program, their sense of program ownership increases, and with it their sense of responsibility, because they have a stake in the program's outcome.

> Change has been difficult for me and I'm still a work in process. But if I can change, you can change, and if you can change, we all can change the way we deal with conflict and violence.
>
> *Project peer leader,*
> *Funderburg Youth Program*

As one example, the organizers initially held a curriculum development workshop that included youth, parents, adults, and community leaders. Following the workshop, four high-school-age youth were brought into the planning process as project peer leaders to ensure that future curriculums both addressed their fears and concerns about dealing with conflict and dealt with the needs of youth.

Project peer leaders also act as teaching assistants. In this role, peer leaders work with the CMG training team to master group facilitation skills while leading discussions and presentations. As peer leaders become proficient in these skills, they play an increasingly prominent role in leading workshops for their peers and middle school youth in the community's clubs, service organizations, churches, and housing districts. They also participate in the community outreach and community-to-school components of the project. Over time, the youth become leaders in partnership with the adults.

Recruitment and Selection of Community Youth. Networking is perhaps the most important key to developing a community-based program. In this project, CMG and UUUM formed an alliance because they shared similar goals in community work. Additionally, UUUM had an existing youth program whose leaders were willing to participate in the project.

Youth were recruited from other organizations such as Boys & Girls Clubs, church programs, court referral programs, and other self-esteem programs for youth in the area. The goal was to reach a broad cross section of community youth. The initial program included 20 participants in addition to the peer leaders.

Community Outreach Component. The community outreach goals of this project are aimed at spreading conflict resolution beyond the First Church in Roxbury to the larger Roxbury community, including the adjoining communities of Dorchester and Mattapan. While in-school programs reach a select audience, this program reaches youth who are not included in traditional school-based conflict resolution programs.

Community-to-School, School-to-Community Component. In this component of the project, CMG and PYN are collaborating to:

◆ Develop a high-school-age conflict resolution and negotiation curriculum.

◆ Train teachers, youth, and community members to teach the curriculum.

◆ Design a model program (including training and curriculum) for replication in other communities.

> This was the most helpful training in conflict resolution and mediation I have ever received. . . . We learned things while we were having fun, and we didn't even know we were learning at the time.
>
> *Streetworker, Boston Police Department*

Conflict resolution training must be comprehensive to be effective in changing the way young people respond to conflict. Therefore, school-based programs need the reinforcement of community-based programs whenever possible to help young people see that conflict resolution measures can be implemented at home and on the street as well as at school. The social network in which youth live and work often presents mixed messages about how to deal proactively with conflict. For example, if youth learn problem-solving processes in the school environment and a competitive "winner-take-all" approach at home or on the street, they will resort to the method that is reinforced and addresses their needs for safety and security.

A community-based program can resolve this dilemma by building on conflict resolution training in school and reinforcing it in other settings. Such a community-based program offers a common vocabulary and common values in the resolution of conflicts.

Community Buy-In and Implications for Replication. Adequate funding and community support are critical to a project of this type. A careful, systematic approach that identifies unmet community needs and builds cooperative support from the ground up in existing programs is crucial. Some of the steps taken to develop the Roxbury Conflict Resolution Project may be useful in evaluating the potential for similar programs elsewhere. The following steps have proved essential to the program:

♦ Conducting a needs assessment for conflict resolution training in the community.

♦ Developing a program that builds on existing programs and fills gaps in conflict resolution training.

♦ Creating and implementing a fundraising plan.

The Community Board Program

Community mediation programs throughout the United States have been at the forefront of bringing conflict resolution services and programming to schools, families, and other youth settings. The Community Board Program (CBP), an organization

established in 1976 to provide neighborhood-based mediation services, began work with San Francisco schools in 1980 at the urging of the Program's volunteer mediators, many of whom were educators. Over time, CBP has developed a whole-school approach that focuses on introducing conflict resolution concepts and skills to as many members of the school community as possible—students, teachers, staff, administrators, and parents. The goal is to change individuals' beliefs about conflict resolution and to provide a system for dealing with conflict.

> Our youth usually deal with violence by reacting to it . . . or giving in to it. Conflict resolution training gives them new choices to deal with it positively. . . . This is exactly the type of training we need in this community.
>
> *Director, Funderburg Youth Program*

This whole-school implementation method corresponds to the Community Board's vision of a harmoniously functioning school community that is able to resolve conflicts, prevent violence, and create a peaceful and equitable atmosphere conducive to learning.[6]

Because youth spend time in both schools and communities, strong connections between the two can benefit them in many ways. Resources can be maximized and services to youth enhanced. When schools and communities are more aware of each other, young people in need of neighborhood-based services receive more effective referrals. The following examples illustrate the Community Board's experience in connecting whole-school and community efforts.

Parental Involvement in Whole-School Work. Parental involvement is an integral component of the Community Board whole-school approach. When students are encouraged and expected to use conflict resolution skills for handling disputes at school, they find it confusing and difficult to return home to a completely different approach. CBP educators express frustration when they hear a student say, "My dad says if somebody hits me, I can hit them back." By incorporating parents into the whole-school project, schools provide youth and parents with effective alternatives for dealing with conflicts peacefully on school grounds and at home.

Parents are encouraged to become involved in a variety of ways. They can begin by creating a core committee—a planning and implementation team comprising teachers, counselors, administrators, students, and parents. Based on the needs of the school, the committee develops an action plan and timeline and oversees the project. Depending on the parents' time and availability, they can help by participating in outreach and publicity, training new student mediators, taking referrals, scheduling mediation sessions, keeping records, facilitating biweekly student mediator meetings, following up cases, and fundraising. Parents can perform some functions with limited training, but certain duties, such as training conflict managers and facilitating biweekly meetings, require intensive training. Parents may join teachers in a 2-day mediation training or attend a series of workshops introducing them to effective family communication and problem-solving skills for use in the home. Some schools create a parent support group to discuss concerns and participate in ongoing skills training and practice.

Parents can assist schools in securing support for a whole-school conflict resolution project by presenting information at parent-teacher association meetings, student and/or parent assemblies, staff meetings, town meetings, and students' classes. A well-informed parent group also serves as an important referral source. It can refer school-related conflicts to the peer mediation program and family- and community-related disputes to a community mediation program. CBP provides free outreach presentations to parent groups on methods for referring cases to the program.

Conflict resolution is what I need and I won't quit until all my friends know about it.

Student, Funderburg Youth Program

The use of conflict management skills by *everyone* in our school community is the key component of our district's efforts to become a multicultural organization.

School superintendent,
Ann Arbor, Michigan

Partnerships Between School and Community Mediation Programs. Partnerships between school-based mediation programs and their community-based counterparts strengthen and benefit both programs. The Community Board of San Francisco and the San Francisco Unified School District foster their strong relationship by using the following strategies:

Sharing Mediators. Youth as young as age 14 are trained to become community mediators. If students are already trained as peer mediators in schools, they only need to participate in an orientation session to join the pool of community mediator volunteers. Such student mediator "sharing" provides important additional resources for the community mediation program. The youth involved learn valuable lessons about effective citizenry and advanced conflict resolution skills.

Cross-Referral System. Even if a school has no peer mediation program, educators can benefit from understanding the sorts of disputes that might be referred to community mediation programs. These include serious incidents involving nonschool youth or a range of parent, educator, and community issues. Certain complex disputes may benefit from both school-based and community-based mediation sessions. Volunteer community mediators and "shared" student peer mediators perform outreach to schools by distributing fliers and making presentations.

Parent-Child Mediation. Youth who may be having attendance or behavioral problems can benefit from a parent-child mediation session from the community mediation program. This service is especially useful for youth who are making the transition from special schools that deal with behavioral difficulties to traditional school settings. School districts that use local community mediation programs may find that these free services are valuable in improving or reestablishing parent-child communication and in helping the family understand rules, behavior, and other mediation issues. This work in turn leads to improved social behavior and academic success.

Training Youth as Trainers. Young people who are trained as trainers to help prepare new mediators for school and community settings are a natural source of talent for peer mediation programs. Students are encouraged to participate in the free neighborhood "Training of Trainers" offered each year. CBP also finds it valuable to have student mediators demonstrate the mediation process as part of its annual community mediation training. This reinforces the benefits and underscores the intergenerational, communitywide aspects of conflict resolution. School and community mediation programs may also want to explore the possibility of compensating mediators and trainers for their training work by marketing the training to youth-serving agencies and other groups in the local community. The Effective Alternatives in Reconciliation Services (EARS) program in the Bronx, New York, has carried out ground-breaking work in this area.

Youth Clubs/Youth Councils. If community and school mediation programs wish to develop joint strategies, they may consider developing a youth club or council. Community mediation programs benefit from youth groups that provide a focus for young mediators, help the program retain youth volunteers, recruit new youth, and provide leadership opportunities for young people to direct the program's youth agenda. A youth club also provides a forum for developing and undertaking special youth-initiated projects. Programs might find it helpful to offer stipends to youth participating in the club or council.

Encouraging Youth-Initiated Cases in Community Mediation. Most programs strongly desire more youth to come forward as "first parties" in the community mediation process. Typically, youth are involved as "second parties," with adults bringing concerns and complaints as the first parties in the case. This situation represents a failure to recognize and respond to the needs of young people. CBP

staff and volunteers are performing outreach to youth-serving organizations and schools to inform students about ways to refer disputes they experience to the local Community Board Program.

Youth-initiated referrals can be increased by developing working relationships with youth-serving organizations involved in efforts to organize youth. The work of these groups can create, in effect, collective first parties of young people for mediation. A youth organization would identify and analyze their issues, such as the lack of afterschool programs or jobs, school policies, and the like; consider who their allies might be; and identify the second parties of the dispute. The needs of young people are better met when youth organizations reach out in a proactive manner to work with community groups to resolve issues before they become conflicts.

Boys & Girls Clubs of America

The Boys & Girls Clubs of America recognizes that many of its young members live in communities where conflict and violence are daily occurrences. Conflicts in the lives of many youth—whether experienced personally or vicariously in school, at home, in the neighborhood, on television, in the movies, or in a computer game—may often lead to or result in violence.

Through a grant from the Bureau of Justice Assistance, Office of Justice Programs, U.S. Department of Justice, the Boys & Girls Clubs of America has developed a violence prevention program that includes the Second Step foundation skills curriculum developed by the Committee for Children. The program teaches club members the problem-solving processes of conflict resolution, anger management, impulse control, and empathy. Also, the Boys & Girls Clubs provides information and training on peer mediation through the Community Board's Conflict Managers program. These programs have been implemented in more than 60 Boys & Girls Clubs located in public housing developments across the country.[7]

Each program presents the message "Conflicts are natural daily occurrences that can have nonviolent resolutions" in a variety of situations to help youth see a range of contexts in which conflicts can arise and be settled without violence. The Boys & Girls Clubs has provided the staff and members of its affiliated clubs across the country with the opportunity to receive training and practice in the peaceful resolution of conflicts. These training programs are also open to parents and other interested adults in the community. The clubs expect that nonviolent skills and strategies for settling interpersonal disputes will begin to be practiced on a regular basis through the many club activities on site and in the home and community.

> These programs have assisted our members in reducing the level of interpersonal violence and in supporting a positive peaceful environment in their respective communities. We look forward to their important message reaching all our youth members in all our Boys & Girls Clubs.
>
> *James D. Cox, Vice President of Urban Services, Boys & Girls Clubs of America*[8]

AmeriCorps Conflict Resolution Training Project

Through a partnership with the National Association for Community Mediation (NAFCM), AmeriCorps, the national service program, has offered training in conflict resolution to its members since September 1995. NAFCM has provided specialized training in the skills and strategies of conflict resolution to more than 9,000 AmeriCorps members in 46 States, American Samoa, and the District of Columbia.[9] Many of the AmeriCorps members who have been trained as a result of this partnership are working directly in kindergarten to grade 12 classrooms, using their training to help teach students conflict resolution and to set up peer mediation programs in schools.

The AmeriCorps trainings have been conducted using NAFCM's national membership network of community mediation centers and a special modular curriculum designed specifically for this project. Each of the three modules of the curriculum focuses on a different aspect of conflict awareness and management. The professional trainers at each center work with the AmeriCorps programs in their area to provide flexible scheduling and a training curriculum that is tailored to the needs, background, and experience of each particular training group. Community mediation centers are also available for further training and technical assistance, because addressing local needs has been the hallmark of their contribution to this national service program.

Community Relations Service

This unique component of the Department of Justice seeks to prevent or resolve community conflicts and tensions arising from actions, policies, and practices perceived to be discriminatory on the basis of race, color, or national origin. The Community Relations Service (CRS) works to bring awareness, education, and action into communities throughout the United States that are experiencing conflicts resulting from a multicultural environment. In these communities, insensitivity to different racial or cultural groups may generate friction and, possibly, disruptions between groups at school. However, the diversity found in school communities offers opportunities for individuals to learn more about one another and to enhance their global awareness.

Conflicts may arise in schools when different student groups "stake out turf" in certain areas of the school—for example, the cafeteria, the resource room, or the athletic fields—or during school dances and sports events; when they leave racist graffiti in the rest rooms or other parts of the campus; and when they form gangs on campus. Conflicts also arise when parents feel that their children's race or ethnicity is not being treated sensitively by teachers, counselors, and administrators.

When disruptions and violence are racially motivated, the shock waves threaten the whole fabric of the community. All who are responsible for school safety and security must keep abreast of demographic changes in the community that will alter the pattern of student interaction in a school. Conflicts that take place outside school, in the community and in the students' neighborhoods, may affect the relationships between students at school. In nearly every major racial disruption in elementary, middle, and secondary schools, warning signs were present well in advance of the incident. The conflict and/or violence might have been avoided had someone recognized that tension was building and taken positive steps to address it. The answers to the following questions will help to identify the warning signs of tension building in the community and school:

♦ What racial and ethnic groups attend the school?

♦ Where do they live in relation to one another?

♦ How do these groups get to and from school?

♦ Do school activities such as sporting events and dances bring together diverse groups that do not ordinarily meet, creating an environment of competition or tension?

♦ What has been the history of interaction among these various groups?

CRS casework shows that in nearly every school disruption based on race, color, or national origin, at least one group perceived that the school's standards were being unfairly applied to them alone. When school administrators and law enforcement officers meet regularly with local community and civil rights groups to discuss community problems, they can develop and support appropriate responses to community conflict through negotiation, mediation, and consensus decisionmaking.

CRS services can also be requested by community groups, school officials, or school support groups such as parent, teacher, and student associations. When a request comes from a recognized party and involves a dispute related to race, CRS initiates its involvement by conducting an assessment of the perceived problem through a series of interviews with the key leaders of the groups involved. After an assessment is completed, CRS meets with the complainant to provide feedback on the perceptions of all parties regarding the problem. At that point, depending on the assessment, CRS may offer to provide a number of services to assist the parties to the dispute to resolve their problem with win-win outcomes for all involved.

To help manage and prevent school and community racial and ethnic disruptions, CRS has developed several programs that can be implemented in individual schools or throughout a school district. Among them are:

♦ **Student conflict resolution teams.** CRS provides training to students in the mediation process and facilitates the establishment of student response teams. These teams are designed to mediate disputes, serve as racial advisory boards, and defuse student-related racial tensions.

♦ **Student problem identification/resolution program.** CRS presents training in this problem-solving approach to address conflict in multiracial schools and districts. The program is a 2-day process in which students develop recommendations and a workplan to improve racial harmony. A principal's student advisory council is also established as an ongoing mechanism to work directly with school administrators and faculty to address racial and ethnic issues both preventively and reactively.

♦ **Conflict management and cultural awareness training for staff.** CRS provides training in conflict management within multicultural settings for administrators, faculty, security personnel, building staff, and bus drivers.

♦ **Management of school disruption and violence.** CRS provides training through a video instruction program covering control of the learning environment, isolation of disputing parties, recognition of the disputants' issues, and implementation of the problem-solving processes of conflict resolution.

♦ **School site coordination.** CRS can assist a school in setting up a committee of appropriate community service providers and agencies to coordinate services and focus resources on the needs and problems of the school and community members.

These CRS programs are offered and implemented in an open and fair manner that gives all members of the school and neighboring community a role in resolving the conflict peacefully. As a result, cooperation increases among the parties and overshadows the differences that initially caused the tensions to build, thereby helping to bring about a win-win outcome for all parties. A list of CRS offices is included in appendix A.

The Arts and Conflict Resolution

The National Endowment for the Arts (NEA), a Federal agency, is dedicated to fostering excellence, diversity, and vitality in the arts in the Nation's communities while helping to broaden their availability and appreciation. NEA encourages use of the arts as a vehicle to address social problems in our communities and schools by supporting programs in arts organizations, local arts agencies, and the Institute for Community Development and the Arts of the National Assembly of Local Arts Agencies.

> The most important learning takes place when several subjects are taught simultaneously in the context of a larger theme—works of art can provide such themes.
>
> *Brent Wilson, School of Visual Arts,*
> *Pennsylvania State University*[10]

The Institute was established to assist local arts agencies, elected and appointed municipal officials, and community leaders in using the arts to address social issues in the community. The Institute's information and technical assistance services provide local arts agencies with the tools necessary to develop innovative community partnerships that use the arts to address social and educational problems. In conjunction with national networks including the Boys & Girls Clubs of America, the U.S. Department of Housing and Urban Development, the National Recreation and Park Association, social service and child advocacy networks, local arts agencies, and national arts service organizations, the Institute has researched more than 600 arts programs for youth at risk.

Many of these programs are reaching disenfranchised youth who are living in violent neighborhoods with little opportunity for healthy activities. Innovative partnerships of arts organizations and social service and youth-serving agencies provide at-risk youth with opportunities to learn conflict resolution education as an integral component in the study and/or practice of music, dance, theater, literature, and the visual arts. These programs are taking place in public housing facilities, schools, recreation centers, churches, libraries, teen centers, Boys & Girls Clubs, local arts and cultural centers, museums, and performing arts organizations. The most effective arts programs recognize the risk factors in the lives of at-risk youth and teach them the abilities and problem-solving processes of conflict resolution to help them live and thrive in a chaotic world. The arts help youth learn to express their joy, disappointment, anger, and fear through the meaningful use of words, music, drawing, sculpture, painting, and performance rather than with fists, knives, and guns.

The arts are uniquely effective in engaging at-risk youth in conflict resolution education. The arts provide creative and emotional outlets that also teach these youth different ways to view the world; foster creativity; teach life skills of effective communication and conflict resolution education; encourage participation among youth who may not be inclined to become engaged; strengthen basic and advanced thinking skills; develop problem-posing and problem-solving processes; and promote better understanding and tolerance between different racial and ethnic groups. The arts reach students who are disenfranchised by providing diverse routes to academic and personal achievement, enhancing self-discipline, teaching perseverance and hard work, and providing gateways to other learning.

The following sections present brief descriptions of arts programs that incorporate conflict resolution education. Resource information on these and other such programs is included in appendix A.

Urban smARTS Program

In many community-based arts programs, conflict resolution training is a critical component to help address an increase in juvenile crime, violence, and gang activity. For example, San Antonio provides funding for Urban smARTS, an afterschool program in 7 schools designed to divert from the juvenile justice system 420 at-risk youth in grades 6 through 8.

The program's partnerships bring together the San Antonio Departments of Arts and Cultural Affairs, the Youth Services Division of Community Initiatives, the Southwest Independent School District, and the law enforcement and higher education communities. The collaboration of the various city agencies and community resources has resulted in a multidisciplinary program that combines innovative arts activities with conflict resolution and social skills training and the delivery of social services. NEA and the Office of Juvenile Justice and Delinquency Prevention (OJJDP) have entered into a collaborative evaluation of this program to determine its effectiveness in decreasing juvenile adjudication and delinquency, increasing academic performance and school attendance, developing the problem-solving processes of conflict resolution, and improving the self-esteem, social skills, and family relationships of at-risk youth.

In the Urban smARTS program, each school is assigned a team of three professional artists, four caseworkers, several volunteers, and one teacher/counselor who work with the youth for the 14-week program. Program goals include:

- Diverting at-risk youth from the juvenile justice system through the arts and conflict resolution education.

- Improving social behavior and skills through the arts and case management teamwork.

- Improving academic performance and commitment to school through the arts.

- Developing art skills and providing art opportunities for performance and exhibitions.

Pathways to Success Program

A collaboration of OJJDP, the Bureau of Justice Assistance, and NEA, the Pathways to Success Program promotes vocational skills, entrepreneurial initiatives, recreation, and arts education during afterschool, weekend, and summer hours by making a variety of opportunities available to at-risk youth. Under this program, 2-year grants have been awarded to five sites. The four listed below include arts and conflict resolution education:

- The Stopover Services (SOS) Playback Arts-Based Delinquency Prevention program in Newport, Rhode Island, provides an afterschool arts program for youth ages 13 to 18 from local public housing. The youth participate in peer-to-peer support and youth/adult partnerships that help build healthy family relationships and a sense of community through the media of visual arts, dance, and drama.

- Project CLEAR (Collaboration Leads to Enhanced Achievement and Resiliency), located in New York City, provides extended day programs to students and their families in two elementary schools with activities including the arts, recreation, and academic tutoring.

- The Anchorage School District and the Out-North Theater have collaborated to work with students to write, produce, and perform plays for the community based on their life experiences.

- The Aspira Youth Sanctuary program addresses the problems of Latino youth ages 12 to 14 residing in migrant camps through the teaching of art, folklore, dance, recreation activities, and parent workshops.

Conflict resolution education is incorporated into each of these programs, because many of the youth live in neighborhoods characterized by poverty, drugs, and crime where even minor disputes often escalate to violence. These programs lend themselves to a discussion of other ways to resolve disputes, which are a normal part of life and will occur naturally during interactions with other individuals, both within and outside the program.

Arts and Prevention Projects

The Department of Education's Safe and Drug-Free Schools Program funded the development of several arts and prevention projects. Developed by the Learning Systems Group, these projects have incorporated many building blocks that strengthened young people's ability to work together and to learn and practice the conflict resolution processes of negotiation, mediation, and consensus decisionmaking. Following are descriptions of several arts and prevention activities.

The Mural Reflecting Prevention project provides educators and youth leaders with resource materials and suggestions on engaging youth in the collaborative process of creating a mural on a drug and violence prevention theme. Through this group work, youth learn negotiation skills and gain an appreciation for different perspectives and for the need to work as a team. In Indianapolis, Indiana, a group of young people worked with a local mural artist, their school, and the city's parks and recreation department to create a powerful and colorful mural on the side of a community park building. Youth in a Dade County, Florida, public housing development worked with a student from a local college of art during spring break to create a mural in their new community center. In contributing to the design and production of the artwork, youth of different ages and ethnic backgrounds developed their patience, listening skills, and creativity and also improved their problem-solving skills. In both cases, the works were celebrated in public events that enabled parents, teachers, and other members of the community to express their support and appreciation of the young people's artwork.

The Art of Prevention project is designed to help teachers expand their school's existing drug prevention curriculum by integrating arts activities centered on prevention themes. The program materials include a 64-page handbook with 14 detailed lesson plans incorporating dance, drama, visual arts, music, language arts, and media arts along with a 13-minute video showing how the arts can be used to teach prevention and prosocial skills. Activities in this resource package cover topics such as decision-making, understanding consequences of actions, and identifying healthy ways to cope with feelings and emotions. The sample activities address these and other drug and violence prevention issues through various art forms and the foundation abilities of conflict resolution education.

Using the arts to teach the message that conflicts can be resolved without violence is exciting and offers many opportunities to bring teachers, parents, and other members of the community into the process. Although varied in scope and focus, these projects share the goal of demonstrating the potential for addressing social problems through the arts. Students learn not only the process of an art form, but also nonviolent alternatives to conflicts. Working together as a team brings results: completed art projects through peaceful conflict resolution.

California Lawyers for the Arts

As an outgrowth of its mediation program, and with support from the National Endowment for the Arts, California Lawyers for the Arts (C.L.A.) uses the arts to address the effect on youth of such social issues as unemployment, violence, and gangs. Through grants from the San Francisco Mayor's Office of Children, Youth, and Their Families and the Office of Community Development, C.L.A. facilitated the placement of 50 low-income youth in summer jobs at 17 San Francisco arts organizations. This project was followed by an afterschool cultural enrichment program coordinated with 6 collaborating arts education providers who are serving more than 600 at-risk youth from diverse ethnic communities. C.L.A. provides the youth with seminars on life skills that include conflict resolution education, communication skills, and job readiness.

Conflict resolution training for youth involved in art enrichment activities is specific for each site and age group. For example, a session recognizing emotions and feelings was developed for 6- to 8-year-olds involved in afterschool movement and performance classes. After a brief exercise using their newly expanded vocabulary to describe emotions and feelings, the children developed and acted out short skits to display what they had learned regarding their own and others' feelings. In contrast, the focus of a session for youth ages 9 to 14 years involved developing a showcase production on how to work together as a group, listen to each other, and use problem-solving processes rather than argue, name-call, and disagree. For older teens placed in summer jobs at arts organizations, a workshop was provided to develop communication and basic employment and negotiation skills through the role-playing of art-related problems. Similar programs are in operation in Southern California and in the Washington, D.C., area.

Notes

1. Sneve, V.D.H. 1987. "Women of the Circle." In H. Thompson, A. Huseboe, and S. Looney (eds.), *A Common Land, A Diverse People*. Sioux Falls, SD: Nordland Heritage Foundation.

2. Brendtro, L., and N. Long. 1993 (Spring). "Violence Begets Violence: Breaking Conflict Cycles." *Journal of Emotional and Behavioral Problems*, p. 5.

3. Ibid.

4. Ibid., pp. 5–6.

5. Beekman, S., and J. Holmes. 1993. *Battles, Hassles, Tantrums & Tears: Strategies for Coping with Conflict and Making Peace at Home*. New York, NY: Hearst Books, William Morrow & Company, Inc., Publishers, p. 90.

6. Wong, P., M. McLaughlin, and M. Moore. 1995 (July). *Evaluation of Phase 1 of the Whole School Conflict Resolution Project*. Final report. Stanford, CA: Stanford University School of Education.

7. The Second Step and Conflict Managers programs are available for use in local Boys & Girls Clubs by contacting the Boys & Girls Clubs National Headquarters (see appendix A under "Community-Based Programs").

8. Cox, J.D. 1996 (May). Personal communication.

9. Contact information for the AmeriCorps Conflict Resolution Training Project and the National Association for Community Mediation is included in appendix A under "Community-Based Programs."

10. Wilson, B. In press. *The Quiet Evolution: Implementing Discipline-Based Art Education in Six Regional Professional Development Consortia*. Santa Monica, CA: Getty Center for Education in the Arts.

Chapter 8: Conflict Resolution Research and Evaluation

Research on conflict situations within schools and on the impact of conflict resolution education programs provides strong support for establishing these programs in schools. Many of the studies conducted to date have focused on mediation programs, which are distinctive and perhaps more prevalent in schools than programs employing one of the other three approaches to conflict resolution education. Because the peaceable classroom and process curriculum approaches integrate conflict resolution education into the normal curriculum, evidence of the success of these approaches has been somewhat difficult to document. However, the positive outcomes associated with mediation programs hold promise that broader based conflict resolution programs that use mediation will be successful as well. Comprehensive studies to evaluate the two peaceable school programs highlighted in chapter 5 are under way.

Early Research

In 1974, DeCecco and Richards published the results of one of the most comprehensive studies on conflict within schools.[2] They interviewed more than 8,000 students and 500 faculty members in more than 60 junior and senior high schools in New York City, Philadelphia, and San Francisco and found that more than 90 percent of the conflicts reported by students were perceived to be either unresolved or resolved in destructive ways. Moreover, negotiation of conflicts was practically nonexistent.

Studies on the Teaching Students To Be Peacemakers Program

More recently, David Johnson and Roger Johnson conducted 11 research studies to examine the

> Research in this field indicates that conflict resolution and mediation programs show positive effects in reducing violence.[1]

effectiveness of the Teaching Students To Be Peacemakers program.[3] Results demonstrate the impact that conflict resolution training programs have on the ability of students to manage their conflicts constructively. Johnson and Johnson conducted carefully controlled studies in inner-city and suburban school districts throughout the United States and Canada. The grade level of the students involved in the research ranged from the 1st through the 10th grades. Two approaches to training in peer mediation were studied. In one, the total student body received the training; in the other, a small group of teachers and students received the training. Students were randomly assigned to one of these approaches, while teachers were rotated across approaches. The following is a summary of the questions asked by these studies and their findings:

◆ *How often do conflicts among students occur, and what are the most commonly occurring conflicts?*

The findings indicated that students engaged in conflicts daily. In the suburban schools studied, the majority of reported conflicts resulted from the possession of and access to resources, choice of available activities, playground issues, and turn-taking. Some conflicts involved physical and verbal aggression. In one urban elementary school studied, the vast majority of conflicts referred to mediation involved physical and verbal violence.

- *What strategies did students use to manage conflicts prior to program training?*

Before training, students generally managed their conflicts in one of three ways: verbal or physical abuse, teacher intervention, or withdrawal from the conflict and the other person. A teacher stated in her log, "Before training, students viewed conflict as fights that always resulted in a winner and a loser. To avoid such an unpleasant situation, they usually placed the responsibility for resolving conflicts on me, the teacher." Students did not know how to engage in problem resolution or integrative negotiations.

- *Did the program training successfully teach students negotiation and mediation procedures?*

After the training ended, students knew the negotiation and mediation procedures and retained this knowledge.

- *Could students apply the negotiation and mediation procedures to conflicts?*

For the three measures used (written responses to conflict scenarios, oral responses to conflict scenarios given in an interview, and role-playing responses to conflict scenarios that were videotaped), students were able to apply the negotiation and mediation procedures to various conflicts.

- *Did students transfer the negotiation and mediation procedures to nonclassroom and nonschool situations?*

The findings showed that students used the negotiation and mediation procedures in the hallways and lunchroom as well as on the playground. They also used the procedures in family settings.

- *Did students rely on "win-lose" strategies or negotiation strategies when presented with an option?*

After completing the program training, students were placed in a negotiation situation that presented the opportunity either to win or to maximize joint outcomes. Although untrained students frequently tried to win, the majority of trained students focused on maximizing joint outcomes.

- *Did the program training increase overall academic achievement?*

In three of the studies, the training was integrated into English literature units. While studying a novel, students learned the negotiation and mediation procedures, which were applied to the dynamics among the major characters. At the conclusion of the unit, students were given an achievement test, and several months later they were retested. The results indicated that the students who received the integrated training earned significantly higher achievement and retention test scores than the students who studied the novel but did not learn conflict resolution procedures.

- *Did the program training result in fewer discipline problems that required teacher and administration management?*

During the studies, the number of discipline problems requiring teacher management decreased by approximately 80 percent, and referrals to the principal were reduced to zero.

- *Did the program training create more positive attitudes toward conflict?*

Untrained students uniformly had negative attitudes toward conflict. After training, students developed more positive attitudes toward conflict. Teachers, administrators, and parents believed that the Teaching Students To Be Peacemakers program was constructive and helpful. Many parents whose children did not participate in the project requested that their children receive the training in the upcoming year. A number of parents also asked if they could receive the training to improve conflict management within the family.

Other Research

Additional assessment of the conflict resolution education field supports the need for conflict resolution programs and legitimizes the contention that effective programs must be based on proven negotiation theory, which can be translated into instructional procedures that educators can use in the classroom. The following items highlight some of the findings of this research:

- The Ohio School Conflict Management Demonstration Project, conducted in 17 schools between 1990 and 1993, improved student attitudes toward conflict, increased understanding of nonviolent problem-solving methods, and enhanced communication skills.[4]

- During the 1992–1993 school year, the Clark County Social Service School Mediation Program in Nevada reduced the amount of conflict among students in the two participating elementary schools and helped prevent fights among students. Peer mediators mediated 163 conflicts and resolved 138 (85 percent). Peer mediators demonstrated a significant increase in conflict management skills, self-esteem, and assertiveness. After the program, the number of teachers who spent less than 20 percent of their time on discipline increased by 18 percent. Similar results were reported for the 1993–1994 school year.[5]

- Evaluation of a mediation program in a suburban Chicago high school indicated positive results. Researchers testing the hypothesis that "mediation is an effective alternative to traditional discipline" found that mediation was more effective than traditional discipline in reducing the number of interpersonal conflicts. The researchers also reported that the majority of disputants and student mediators were very satisfied with all aspects of the mediation.[6]

- Evaluation of the impact of the Resolving Conflict Creatively Program (RCCP) in four multiracial, multi-ethnic school districts in New York City showed that 84 percent of teachers who responded to a survey reported positive changes in classroom climate; 71 percent reported moderate or significant decreases in physical violence in the classroom; and 66 percent observed less name-calling and fewer verbal insults. Similar percentages of teachers characterized students as demonstrating improved perspective-taking skills, a greater willingness to cooperate, and more "caring behavior." More than 98 percent of respondents said that the mediation component gave children an important tool for handling conflicts. Other changes reported included spontaneous usage of conflict resolution skills, improved self-esteem and sense of empowerment, increased awareness and articulation of feelings, and greater acceptance of differences.[7]

- Five of the six New York City high schools participating in Project S.M.A.R.T. (School Mediator Alternative Resolution Team) experienced a 45- to 70-percent reduction in suspensions for fighting during the program's first year of operation.[8]

- An evaluation report of the Mediation in Schools Program of the New Mexico Center for Dispute Resolution (NMCDR) reported that teachers in program schools noticed less violence and harmful behavior among students, whereas teachers in nonprogram schools noticed more violence. One Albuquerque elementary school principal reported that "We were having 100 to 150 fights every month on the playground before we started the program. By the end of the school year, we were having maybe 10 [fights]." Other elementary schools using the same NMCDR program reported that playground fighting had been reduced to such an extent that peer mediators found themselves out of a job.[9]

Program teachers frequently used positive, noncoercive conflict resolution strategies—especially mediation—when responding to "hurtful" behavior among students. On the other hand, nonprogram teachers often used coercive, win-lose, adult-authored strategies—especially detention and referrals to the principal's office—when responding to problem behavior.

Students successfully operated the peer mediation process initiated through the program. In a total of more than 2,300 mediations, only 250 required adult intervention. Students trained as mediators had clearer definitions of mediation and conflict resolution strategies and skills than their untrained peers. Untrained students did not fully understand the benefits of win-win situations or specific and creative conflict resolution strategies. In addition, untrained students neither showed the levels of self-esteem and confidence nor felt as positive about school as trained students. The amount of time staff members in program schools spent handling conflicts was reduced, as was the number of violent incidents among students.[10]

♦ The International Center for Cooperation and Conflict Resolution at Columbia Teachers College in New York initiated a conflict resolution research project at a New York City alternative high school. Results from the program indicated positive effects on the students trained in conflict resolution. These students improved their ability to manage conflicts while experiencing more social support and less victimization from others than before. Improving relations with others led to increased self-esteem, more positive feelings of well-being, and decreased feelings of anxiety and depression. Along with more self-esteem, students perceived themselves as having greater personal control over their fates. The increased sense of personal control and positive feelings of well-being led to improved academic performance. Indirect evidence suggested that exposure to the training also enhanced work readiness and performance.[11]

♦ The Harvard Graduate School of Education is systematically evaluating the impact of the Program for Young Negotiators (PYN). Preliminary findings from the evaluation team suggest that the majority of participating students are learning and using the basic techniques taught by the program. Most interviewed participants were able to discuss in depth the importance of "talking it out" to avoid fights and accomplish goals. They stated that the program taught them that they have options for dealing with conflicts with peers, parents, and teachers. Reports from parents and teachers confirmed that the youth did change their behavior and handled conflicts without resorting to violence. Participants also stated that the program taught them skills for how to get ahead in life, such as making plans and learning how to state what they want and what they really mean. The majority also described the experience as fun because it used games and role-plays. This point is important, because the fun experience keeps students engaged in the training process and facilitates their recall of the basic messages.

Interviews revealed that most students could cite concrete examples of using their negotiation skills with peers and parents. Several students reported that the practice of negotiation at home surprised their parents, but generally the parents responded positively to the switch from arguing, complaining, and resisting to negotiating. Parents have reported that the use of negotiation has created opportunities for positive parent-child discussions.

Teachers who taught the curriculum evaluated the training as useful to their work both in the PYN and in their other classes. They reported that the curriculum content and structure—particularly the role-plays and negotiation games—promoted important discussion of topics such as decisionmaking, planning for the future, and conflict resolution. The teachers also reported seeing changes in the communication and conflict resolution styles of many of the students participating in the program. The benefits cited by the six principals interviewed included an improvement in the students' ability to talk through disagreements and an opportunity for teachers to think through their own conflict management style.[12]

♦ In 1991, the Peace Education Foundation (PEF) Conflict Resolution and Peer Mediation programs were initiated throughout the region II public schools in Dade County, Florida. School staff were trained to establish classroom-based and schoolwide student mediation programs and to incorporate conflict resolution instruction into school curriculums.

A review of mediator reports showed that 86 percent of mediated conflicts were resolved. Student Case Management Systems, a system used to report incidents, showed a significant reduction in the rate of referrals for general disruptive behavior in the elementary schools that had the highest levels of implementation. Furthermore, the PEF conflict resolution model affected student attitudes toward resolving conflicts positively. Student surveys indicated that those who received training were more willing to resolve conflict situations through actions other than threats and violence.[13]

In 1994, staff teams from seven alternative and two middle schools with a high percentage of at-risk students received training in the PEF Conflict Resolution model. Postintervention surveys showed that students significantly changed their attitudes toward conflict after learning the PEF model. Students were more inclined to explain, reason, compromise, or share in an effort to resolve their conflicts. Students were less likely to involve authority figures or to use aggression and threats when resolving conflicts. Additional surveys indicated that teachers felt more respected and less frustrated after the implementation of the PEF model.[14]

◆ Evaluations of a conflict resolution initiative in the Palm Beach County school district showed a considerable reduction in student referrals and suspensions. For example, after the Safe School Center initiated a conflict resolution program using the PEF curriculum at Spady Elementary School, the number of referrals at the school dropped from 124 between September and December 1992 to 5 during the same period in 1994.

Between January and June 1995, the Safe School Center sponsored 49 Fighting Fair for Families workshops throughout the Palm Beach County school district. Parents who attended one of these workshops, which used PEF materials, noticed favorable results. In a 2-month followup survey of 163 participants, 79 percent reported improving how conflicts were handled at home, 76 percent reported improving how feelings were treated at home, and 70 percent reported improving how people listened to each other at home. In addition, 80 percent still displayed the Rules for Fighting Fair poster in their homes.[15]

◆ During the 1992–1993 school year, a middle school with an enrollment of more than 700 students in Orange County, North Carolina, initiated a conflict resolution program that included a combination of components from various conflict resolution projects. Nine teachers and 391 sixth-grade students were taught about conflict resolution through lectures, discussion groups, and role-playing. The students were

taught about individuality, anger, and power. The project also taught the students the PEF Rules for Fighting Fair from the same Fighting Fair curriculum used in the Florida study described above. Twenty-six students were selected by their peers to be trained in peer mediation. After four 4-hour training sessions, the peer mediators provided mediation when needed. Mediation sessions lasted up to 1 hour and took place in a counselor's office or a conference room. Adults were nearby if requested.

The outcomes of this conflict resolution project were significant. The sixth-grade students' behavior patterns exhibited a marked change from the 1991–1992 school year to the 1992–1993 school year. Disciplinary referrals to the principal's office dropped from 150 to 27 (82 percent), in-school suspensions decreased from 52 to 30 (42 percent), and out-of-school suspensions decreased from 40 to 1 (97 percent). The reduced number of disciplinary actions suggests that the conflict resolution project had a beneficial effect, but it is not clear whether the 1991–1992 school year was atypical with regard to behavior problems, and it is not known whether the decreases represented specific disciplinary actions or all kinds of actions. Nevertheless, the reductions are impressive.[16]

◆ The Mediation Project of the Public Justice Department of St. Mary's University in San Antonio, Texas, has provided middle and high school students with conflict resolution training through a school-university-community project. Preliminary studies of the first schools trained have shown significant reductions in disciplinary problems and in student violence on school campuses. Smithson Valley Middle School recorded a 57-percent decrease in disciplinary actions during the first year of its peer-based mediation program.[17]

◆ Through the Lawyers Adopt-a-School Program of the American Bar Association, Section of Dispute Resolution, lawyers have successfully adopted several schools in Montgomery County, Maryland: Bradley Hills Elementary School, Springbrook High School, Francis Scott Key Middle School, and White Oak Middle School.

After 1 year of operation, the program reported the following middle school results: office referrals were reduced from 384 to 67, suspensions for disruptive behavior were reduced from 54 to 14, and fights were reduced from 52 to 9. The disputes were usually mediated during lunch break, with the average mediation lasting 22 minutes. As a result of the program's success, the Lawyers Adopt-a-School Program is being replicated in sites across the country.[18]

Further research and evaluation of conflict resolution education programs are needed for comprehensive identification of the strengths and weaknesses of program elements and strategies. Research should address cultural issues and developmentally appropriate practices for conflict resolution education. The body of research on conflict resolution education is expected to grow along these lines. This type of information will be invaluable to program administrators and practitioners. The findings will help strengthen the adoption and implementation of conflict resolution education and foster sustained support in schools, youth-serving organizations, and community and juvenile justice settings. In addition, data from future studies may illuminate lessons learned from successful use of conflict resolution skills by young people in all aspects of their lives.

Implications of Research on Risk Factors and Resilience

Research on social development indirectly supports the value of conflict resolution education, particularly for at-risk youth. Some youth whose social and economic circumstances place them at risk for violent or self-destructive behavior are able to avoid outcomes such as dropping out of school, using drugs, getting pregnant, or participating in gang activities. These youth have been identified as possessing "resilience" derived from factors such as a sense of belonging, the ability to communicate effectively, flexibility, and good problem-solving skills. Resilience has been defined as "the ability to overcome the effects of [a] high-risk environment and to develop social competence despite exposure to severe stress."[19] Resilient youth are able to overcome risk factors such as inadequate bonding or caring, low expectations, a negative school climate, academic failure, and economic or social deprivation. Table 3 lists the characteristics found in resilient children.

> "Mom, can I tell you something? I'm worried. All of the boys I grew up with are dead. I lie awake at night and think about it. What am I supposed to do?" The question was from a thirteen-year-old boy in New Orleans and caused his mother to realize that, of a group of six-year-olds who started school together seven years earlier, only her son was still living. All the others had met violent deaths.[20]

Risk Factors for Violent and Antisocial Behavior

In their work on social development, Catalano and Hawkins have identified four major categories of risk factors that consistently predict delinquent or antisocial behavior among youth. Figure 6 lists these risk factors identified in longitudinal studies as predictors of health and behavior problems. The specific problems predicted by each risk factor are checked in the figure.[21]

Although the presence of these risk factors does not guarantee violent or antisocial behavior in the future, it increases the probability of such behavior. Awareness of risk factors can alert teachers, counselors, and others to the need for early intervention. For example, bullying is an early indicator of life-long antisocial problems, so intervening at the preschool and early elementary school levels is a logical step to help prevent these outcomes.

Protective Factors

Protective factors are conditions or influences that mitigate risk factors and promote resilience. On the basis of the evidence concerning protective factors, Hawkins, Doucek, and Lishner have formulated a theory of social development that identifies

Table 3: Characteristics of Resilient Children

Social Competence	Problem-Solving Skills	Sense of Autonomy
◆ Responsiveness to others. ◆ Conceptual and intellectual flexibility. ◆ Caring for others. ◆ Good communication skills. ◆ Sense of humor.	◆ Ability to apply abstract thinking. ◆ Ability to engage in reflective thought. ◆ Critical reasoning skills. ◆ Ability to develop alternative solutions in frustrating situations.	◆ Positive sense of independence. ◆ Emerging feelings of efficacy. ◆ High self-esteem. ◆ Impulse control. ◆ Planning and goal setting. ◆ Belief in the future.

Source: Benard, B. 1993 (November). "Fostering Resiliency in Kids." *Educational Leadership*, pp. 44–48. Reprinted with permission of the Association for Supervision and Curriculum Development.

bonding—the feeling of being connected to others—as the overarching protective factor in the development of healthy behavior. Early in life, resilient children often establish positive adult and peer relationships that bond them to family, school, and community. Hawkins and colleagues outline three protective processes necessary for the development of strong bonds: opportunities, skills, and recognition.[22]

◆ **Opportunities.** Children must have the opportunity to contribute to their family, school, and community. The goal is to provide children with meaningful, challenging, developmentally appropriate opportunities that help them feel responsible and significant. Research shows that bonding to school occurs when instructional methods emphasize proactive classroom management, interactive teaching, and cooperative learning.

◆ **Skills.** Students need opportunities to learn the cognitive and social skills that are necessary to solve problems and interact with others. If they lack the appropriate skills, children will experience frustration and failure and their opportunities to bond will be limited.

◆ **Recognition.** Children feel potent and powerful when their contributions are valued by their peers, teachers, and families. Children must be recognized for their capabilities and for their participation.

The Relation Between Resilience and Conflict Resolution

The relation between resilience and conflict resolution is clear and significant. The characteristics of resilience listed in table 3 are essentially the same as the foundation abilities of conflict resolution (orientation, perception, emotion, communication, and creative and critical thinking).[23] In developing a conflict resolution education program, a school creates an environment that fosters the development of resilience in children in three ways. First, resolving conflicts in principled ways promotes and preserves relationships, thereby facilitating the bonding that is essential to the development of resilience. Second, conflict resolution education develops resilience by showing youth that they can control their behavior by making choices that satisfy their needs. Finally, in offering youth the opportunity to resolve conflicts peacefully, conflict resolution education sends an empowering message of trust and perceived capability in which the characteristics of resilience can thrive.

Figure 6: Risk Factors for Health and Behavior Problems

Risk Factor	Substance Abuse	Delinquency	Teenage Pregnancy	School Dropout	Violence
Community					
Availability of drugs	✔				
Availability of firearms		✔			✔
Community laws and norms favorable toward drug use, firearms, and crime	✔	✔			✔
Media portrayals of violence					✔
Transitions and mobility	✔	✔		✔	
Low neighborhood attachment and community organization	✔	✔			✔
Extreme economic deprivation	✔	✔	✔	✔	✔
Family					
Family history of the problem behavior	✔	✔	✔	✔	
Family management problems	✔	✔	✔	✔	✔
Family conflict	✔	✔	✔	✔	✔
Favorable parental attitudes and involvement in the problem behavior	✔	✔			✔
School					
Early and persistent antisocial behavior	✔	✔	✔	✔	✔
Academic failure beginning in elementary school	✔	✔	✔	✔	✔
Lack of commitment to school	✔	✔	✔	✔	
Individual/Peer					
Rebelliousness	✔	✔		✔	
Friends who engage in the problem behavior	✔	✔	✔	✔	✔
Favorable attitudes toward the problem behavior	✔	✔	✔	✔	
Early initiation of the problem behavior	✔	✔	✔	✔	✔
Constitutional factors	✔	✔			✔

Adolescent Problem Behaviors

Source: Catalano, R., and J.D. Hawkins. 1995. *Communities That Care: Risk-Focused Prevention Using the Social Development Strategy.* Seattle, WA: Developmental Research and Programs, Inc., p. 10. Reprinted with the permission of the authors and of Developmental Research and Programs, Inc.

Notes

1. Hechinger, F. 1994. "Saving Youth From Violence." *Carnegie Quarterly* 39(1):7.

2. DeCecco, J., and A. Richards. 1974. *Growing Pains: Uses of School Conflict.* New York, NY: Aberdeen Press.

3. Johnson, D., and R. Johnson. 1995. "Teaching Students To Be Peacemakers: Results of Five Years of Research." *Peace and Conflict: Journal of Peace Psychology* 1(4):417–438. See also Johnson, D., and R. Johnson. 1995. *Teaching Students To Be Peacemakers.* 3d edition. Edina, MN: Interaction Book Company.

4. Ohio Commission on Dispute Resolution and Conflict Management. 1994. *Conflict Management in Schools: Sowing Seeds for a Safer Society.* Columbus, OH: Ohio Commission on Dispute Resolution and Conflict Management, p. 11.

5. Carpenter, J. 1993, 1994. *Clark County Social Service School Mediation Program Evaluation Reports.* Clark County, NV: Clark County Social Service.

6. Tolsen, E.R., S. McDonald, and A. Moriarty. 1990. *Peer Mediation Among High School Students: A Test of Effectiveness.* Chicago, IL: Center for Urban Research and Development, University of Illinois.

7. *Resolving Conflict Creatively Program: 1988–89 Summary of Significant Findings.* 1990 (May). New York, NY: Metis Associates, Inc.

8. Lam, J. 1989. *The Impact of Conflict Resolution Programs on Schools: A Review and Synthesis of the Evidence.* 2d edition. Amherst, MA: National Association for Mediation in Education.

9. Smith, M. 1996. "Strategies to Reduce School Violence: The New Mexico Center for Dispute Resolution." In A.M. Hoffman (ed.), *Schools, Violence, and Society.* Westport, CT: Praeger, p. 256.

10. Carter, S. 1994. *Evaluation Report for the New Mexico Center for Dispute Resolution: Mediation in the Schools Program, 1993–1994 School Year.* Albuquerque, NM: New Mexico Center for Dispute Resolution.

11. Deutsch, M., V. Mitchell, Q. Zhang, N. Khattri, L. Tepavac, E.A. Weitzman, and R. Lynch. 1992. *The Effects of Training in Cooperative Learning and Conflict Resolution in an Alternative High School.* New York, NY: Columbia University.

12. Nakkula, M., and C. Nikitopoulos. 1996 (May). *Preliminary Evaluation Findings for the Fall 1995 Implementation of the Program for Young Negotiators.* Harvard University Graduate School of Education, Cambridge, MA.

Photocopy. Note: The findings in this report are extracted from a longer evaluation document that is updated monthly and is available from the Program for Young Negotiators (see appendix A for contact information).

13. Hanson, M.K. 1994 (Fall). "A Conflict Resolution/Student Mediation Program: Effects on Student Attitudes and Behaviors." *ERS Spectrum* 12(4):9–14.

14. Hanson, M.K. 1995 (September). Conflict Resolution Training at Selected Middle and Alternative Schools, 1994–1995, Dade County Public Schools, Office of Educational Accountability (personal communication).

15. Lewis, R. 1996 (May). Results from a telephone survey conducted by the Safe School Center, 330 Forrest Hill Boulevard, Suite B–121, West Palm Beach, FL 33406 (personal communication).

16. Powell, K.M., L. Muir-McClain, and L. Halasyamani. 1995. "A Review of Selected School-Based Conflict Resolution and Peer Mediation Projects." *Journal of School Health* 65(10):426–431.

17. Leal, R. 1993 (August). "The Next Generation of Campus Mediation Programs." Paper presented at the regional meeting of the Society of Professionals in Dispute Resolution, San Antonio, Texas. See also Leal, R., P. Hollis, and D. Cole. 1996 (April). "A Collaborative School-University Mediation Program." Paper presented at the Second Annual Alternatives to Violence Conference, Sam Houston University, Galveston, Texas.

18. Dabson, J. 1994. "Internal Report: Youth At Risk." Washington, D.C.: American Bar Association, Section of Dispute Resolution, p. 3.

19. Wright, N.D. 1994. *From Risk to Resilience: The Role of Law-Related Education.* Chicago, IL: American Bar Association, p. 2.

20. Hechinger, p. 1.

21. Catalano, R., and J.D. Hawkins. 1995. *Communities That Care: Risk-Focused Prevention Using the Social Development Strategy.* Seattle, WA: Developmental Research and Programs, Inc., p. 10.

22. Hawkins, J.D., H. Doucek, and D. Lishner. 1988 (Spring). "Changing Teaching Practices in Mainstream Classrooms To Improve Bonding and Behavior of Low Achievers." *American Research Journal* 25(1):31–50.

23. Bodine, R., and D. Crawford. In press. *Developing Emotional Intelligence Through Classroom Management: Creating Responsible Learners in Our Schools and Effective Citizens for Our World.* Champaign, IL: Research Press, Inc.

Chapter 9: Developmentally Appropriate Practice

This chapter presents a developmental sequence of behavioral expectations associated with the foundation abilities and practice of conflict resolution. The expectations are reasonable for the general age groupings if learning opportunities and ample practice have been provided. This developmental sequence (tables 4 and 5) is based on an examination of the literature in the field of conflict resolution and an examination of school practices that offer conflict resolution training to students. It is intended to provide guideposts for developing proficiency in conflict resolution. It is not intended to cover every aspect of conflict resolution.

As with any educational program, the outcome of a conflict resolution program will be optimal when it is designed to meet the specific needs of the students enrolled in it. Best practice suggests that to develop the proficiency expected at any given age level, students must already have developed the proficiency expected at all the preceding age levels. Students cannot be expected to use behaviors they have not yet been taught. For example, if a conflict resolution program is initiated for high school students, that program must address more than just the developmental sequence targeted to high school students. Because all students cannot be presumed to have developed proficiency in the foundation abilities and problem-solving processes of conflict resolution, the program must provide them with age-appropriate opportunities to learn and demonstrate the proficiencies that appear in the sequence for all prior age levels. The developmental continuum in tables 4 and 5 suggests what to assess to determine a youth's proficiency level.

Finally, any definitive developmental sequencing should be subordinate to consideration of the individual. Although every individual experiences conflict, each individual enters and exits conflicts differently.

> The test of a first-rate intelligence is the ability to hold two opposed ideas in the mind at the same time, and still retain the ability to function.
>
> *F. Scott Fitzgerald*

Age-Appropriate Instruction

If conflict resolution is to be taught successfully, the curriculum and program must include practice both in building the foundation abilities and in using the problem-solving processes. First, students need to learn the intellectual framework for conflict resolution and to develop the tools to think systematically about conflict. They must then be given the opportunity to practice these skills in a real-life context. The emphasis must be on practice. To complete the transition from learning about the processes of conflict resolution to using those processes in actual situations, the processes must be "overlearned." Sufficient and diverse age-appropriate activities that give students the opportunity for practice, evaluation, and further practice are crucial to the success of any conflict resolution program.

The following learning tools and activities are suggested for use at each developmental level:

♦ **Early childhood education (kindergarten through grade 2):** Using stories, role-plays, games that promote cooperation, classroom projects, field trips involving the greater community, activity cards, posters, puppets, skits, demonstrations, and activities that encourage interaction with older children.

◆ **Elementary school (grades 3–5):** Integrating problem-solving analysis into the standard curriculum and using role-plays, classroom projects and class meetings, school-based peer mediation programs, videos, games, school assemblies, classroom demonstrations, and student presentations to parent and community groups.

◆ **Middle school (grades 6–8):** Teaching students to train younger students in the problem-solving strategies of conflict resolution by helping them to negotiate or by facilitating consensus decision-making sessions, integrating conflict resolution into the regular school curriculum, holding school assembly demonstrations, having students create role-play exercises, having students perform informational demonstrations or skits for the parents and community, and having students provide actual conflict resolution services to community organizations.

◆ **High school (grades 9–12):** Establishing peer mediation programs; teaching students to train other students as peer mediators; holding school assemblies and demonstrations; creating role-play exercises; producing videos; having students and school professionals provide conflict resolution training to the community; letting students assist schools with the development of conflict resolution programs for younger children; having students serve as mediators or facilitators for community programs for younger children, senior citizens, and other community-based groups; and having students serve as mediators in local school and community disputes. In the departmental framework of most secondary schools, conflict resolution education can be offered as a specific course in the general curriculum, integrated into other courses, or organized as a special instructional unit within appropriate subject matter courses.

In summary, the developmental sequence presented in tables 4 and 5 is valid for educating youth, regardless of the setting. If the youth has not developed the proficiency expected of someone younger, that proficiency must be developed through age-appropriate instruction and activities.

Table 4: Age-Appropriate Sequence for Acquiring the Foundation Abilities of Conflict Resolution

Early Childhood to Grade 2	Grades 3–5	Grades 6–8	Grades 9–12
Orientation Abilities			
◆ Understands that having conflicts is natural and knows that involvement in conflicts is all right. ◆ Knows that conflicts can be solved through cooperation. ◆ Views peace as a desired condition and identifies several peacemaking and peacebreaking behaviors. ◆ Differentiates between prejudice and a dislike.	◆ Understands that conflict is inevitable and that it can be a positive force for growth. ◆ Understands that conflicts can become better or worse, depending on the chosen response. ◆ Understands and recognizes soft, hard, and principled responses to conflicts. ◆ Participates in cooperative endeavors. ◆ Recognizes prejudice in self and in the actions of others. ◆ Understands own behavior in terms of the need for belonging, power, freedom, and fun. ◆ Understands peace as a personal action and differentiates between peacemaking and peacebreaking behaviors in self and others.	◆ Recognizes that the sources of conflict and the problem-solving processes of conflict resolution are applicable to all types of conflicts—interpersonal, intergroup, and international. ◆ Diagnoses conflicts appropriately and selects conflict resolution strategies for conflicts in various settings (such as school, home, and neighborhood). ◆ Exhibits effective responses to another person who, in a shared conflict, chooses a soft or hard response. ◆ Takes action to inform when prejudice is displayed. ◆ Suggests a peacemaking action as an alternative to a displayed peacebreaking action.	◆ Maintains various good working relationships with parents, family, siblings, boyfriends, girlfriends, teachers, and bosses. ◆ Analyzes conflict in the context of a present relationship and uses an appropriate problem-solving strategy. ◆ Recognizes patterns in his or her responses to conflict and strives for positive growth and change in those patterns. ◆ Understands that conflict resolution skills are life skills. ◆ Confronts prejudice effectively in self and others and in the school as an institution. ◆ Promotes equal access and opportunity on many fronts. ◆ Seeks diverse and multicultural experiences and relationships. ◆ Works actively to promote peace in the school and in the community.
Perception Abilities			
◆ Accepts that he or she is not always "right." ◆ Accepts that others may see things differently. ◆ Describes a conflict from own perspective and from the perspective of others. ◆ Withholds blame.	◆ Identifies and checks own assumptions about a situation. ◆ Understands how others perceive words and actions. ◆ Empathizes and accepts the feelings and perceptions of others. ◆ Analyzes a conflict from the perspective of unmet basic psychological needs. ◆ Understands friendships and good working relationships and strives to build and maintain them. ◆ Understands the effects of blaming and accusing behaviors and chooses not to act in that manner.	◆ Recognizes the limitations of own perceptions and understands that selective filters affect seeing and hearing. ◆ Identifies and checks assumptions that self and others make about a situation. ◆ Possesses a rudimentary understanding of how problem-solving strategies can be influenced. ◆ Recognizes the prevalence and glamorization of violence in society. ◆ Recognizes that conflicts can escalate into violence.	◆ Critically analyzes own perceptions and modifies understanding as new information emerges. ◆ Articulates how own words, actions, and emotions are perceived by others. ◆ Analyzes how perceptions of others relate to probable intent or purpose. ◆ Understands how problem-solving strategies can be influenced and regularly chooses to exercise positive influence. ◆ Prevents escalation of conflicts, even with adults. ◆ Helps others recognize the potential for violence and for nonviolent conflict resolution.

Table 4: Age-Appropriate Sequence for Acquiring the Foundation Abilities of Conflict Resolution (continued)

Early Childhood to Grade 2	Grades 3–5	Grades 6–8	Grades 9–12
Emotion Abilities			
◆ Knows that feeling anger, frustration, and fear is all right. ◆ Controls anger. ◆ Expresses feelings in language that expands beyond happy, sad, glad, or mad. ◆ Hears and acknowledges the feelings of others. ◆ Does not react to emotional outbursts of others by elevating own emotional response.	◆ Understands own emotions. ◆ Understands that others have emotional responses and that those responses may be different from his or her own. ◆ Expresses emotions effectively and appropriately. ◆ Disagrees without being disagreeable.	◆ Takes responsibility for emotions. ◆ Accepts and validates emotions and perceptions of others. ◆ Possesses effective strategies for "cool down" and uses them at appropriate times.	◆ Remains calm and focused on problem solving when confronted by a strong emotional display from another person, including an adult. ◆ Prevents conflict escalation and violence effectively by using communication-based conflict resolution strategies.
Creative Thinking Abilities			
◆ Describes what is wanted and why it is wanted. ◆ Generates ideas for solving a problem. ◆ Improves a simple idea.	◆ Distinguishes between positions and interests. ◆ Identifies interests beyond own position in any situation. ◆ Separates inventing options from making decisions. ◆ Identifies mutual and compatible interests and creates behavioral options to satisfy those interests.	◆ Understands that underlying interests, not positions, define the problem in conflict situations. ◆ Understands that multiple, unclear, or conflicting interests often coexist. ◆ Understands and uses analytical tools to diagnose problems. ◆ Uses problem solving for conflicting as well as common or compatible interests.	◆ Evaluates and reconciles positions and interests of self and others in most situations. ◆ Prioritizes interests and develops a strategy for working toward agreement, focusing on easier issues first (those of mutual concern) and more difficult issues last (those of conflicting concerns). ◆ Articulates mutual interests and reconciles conflicting interests. ◆ Switches perspectives to generate new options. ◆ Manages brainstorming effectively, separates inventing from deciding, and advocates options for mutual gain. ◆ Brainstorms multiple options in any situation, improving, refining, embellishing, and expanding on current options. ◆ Uses analytical tools to diagnose problems, develop new approaches, and evaluate those approaches.

Table 4: Age-Appropriate Sequence for Acquiring the Foundation Abilities of Conflict Resolution (continued)

Early Childhood to Grade 2	Grades 3–5	Grades 6–8	Grades 9–12
Communication Abilities			
◆ Listens without interruption while another person describes an incident and summarizes what that person has said. ◆ Describes an incident intelligibly using "I" statements. ◆ Uses questions such as "How did that make you feel?" and "What happened next?" ◆ Answers questions about a conflict. ◆ Uses a conflict resolution vocabulary (such as "interests," "options," "brainstorm," "negotiate," and "point of view").	◆ Summarizes the facts and feelings of another person's perspective. ◆ Asks specific, clarifying questions to gather more information. ◆ Uses appropriate problem-solving phraseology (e.g., "and" rather than "but" and "we" instead of "me" or "you"). ◆ Makes "I" statements rather than "you" statements when expressing perspective. ◆ Recognizes nonverbal communication by self and by others, especially communication related to feelings. ◆ Communicates desire for cooperative working relationships.	◆ Uses summarizing and clarifying to defuse anger and deescalate conflict. ◆ Withholds judgment and listens to persuasive discussions. ◆ Is productively persuasive. ◆ Tests understanding, listens to understand, and speaks to be understood. ◆ Reframes own statements using unbiased and less inflammatory language.	◆ Summarizes positions and interests of others in conflict situations efficiently and accurately. ◆ Acknowledges the validity of emotions and perspectives of others. ◆ Reframes statements of others, removing biased or inflammatory messages to capture the underlying meaning. ◆ Expresses interests explicitly. ◆ Uses clarifying questions to uncover hidden interests of others. ◆ Possesses a conflict resolution vocabulary (e.g., "position," "interests," "options," "alternatives," "consensus," "commitment," "legitimacy," and "brainstorm") and uses it appropriately.
Critical Thinking Abilities			
◆ Chooses from multiple ideas. ◆ Understands when something is fair to self and fair to another person. ◆ Explains why something is not fair. ◆ Expresses a realistic and workable plan for resolving a conflict. ◆ Understands the meaning of committing to a plan and being trustworthy.	◆ Evaluates realistically the risks and consequences of "flight or fight" in conflict. ◆ Identifies best self-help alternative in a conflict situation. ◆ Chooses to work toward mutual fairness in resolving a dispute rather than to accomplish self-imposed will. ◆ Evaluates interests of self and others according to fairness standards. ◆ Crafts win-win resolutions. ◆ Specifies clear agreement by stating who, what, when, and how.	◆ Challenges assumptions about what is possible. ◆ Thinks about short- and long-term consequences of proposed options. ◆ Negotiates without conceding. ◆ Identifies outside standards and criteria for fairness (such as legal standards and school rules) when evaluating interests and solutions. ◆ Recognizes the efficacy of committing only to solutions that are fair, realistic, and workable. ◆ Endeavors to fulfill commitments.	◆ Uses problem-solving processes when engaging in difficult conversations. ◆ Speculates as to best alternatives to negotiated agreement for self and others. ◆ Analyzes ways to improve best alternatives to negotiated agreement. ◆ Analyzes willingness and ability of self and other person to honor a plan of action in any situation. ◆ Identifies uncontrollable factors that might impact the ability of the parties to fulfill an agreement. ◆ Identifies external standards of fairness and uses those to resolve conflicts. ◆ Honors commitments and encourages others to do the same.

Table 5: Age-Appropriate Sequence for Acquiring the Problem-Solving Processes of Conflict Resolution

Early Childhood to Grade 2	Grades 3–5	Grades 6–8	Grades 9–12
Negotiation Process			
◆ Cooperates with a peer in unassisted problem solving—each cools off, tells what happened, imagines ways to problem-solve, and chooses a solution. ◆ Participates in a negotiation session coached by an adult or older child.	◆ Manages the negotiation process without assistance.	◆ Performs principled negotiation with peers and adults. ◆ Involves a peer who has little or no conflict resolution training in the negotiation process. ◆ Understands that nearly every interaction is a negotiation. ◆ Teaches younger students the negotiation process.	◆ Negotiates with difficult parties effectively. ◆ Teaches negotiation process to peers and adults. ◆ Enjoys negotiation process.
Mediation Process			
◆ Participates in a mediation facilitated by an adult or older student mediator.	◆ Participates in the mediation process facilitated by another student or an adult. ◆ Serves as a peer mediator in a classroom program or a schoolwide program.	◆ Mediates disputes among peers. ◆ Co-mediates disputes between peers and adults. ◆ Coaches younger students and peers as they learn to mediate.	◆ Mediates an array of disputes involving various disputants. ◆ Trains others in the mediation process.
Consensus Decisionmaking Process			
◆ Engages in group problem-solving discussions and processes facilitated by a teacher or other adult.	◆ Participates in classroom sessions designed to resolve group conflicts and problems.	◆ Manages consensus problem-solving sessions for classroom groups of younger students. ◆ Manages consensus decisionmaking in a small group of peers (such as classroom work group or student council committee).	◆ Manages consensus problem solving in various groups. ◆ Facilitates consensus decisionmaking as a member of a group.

Chapter 10: Establishing Conflict Resolution Education Programs

Although there is no set formula for how to implement conflict resolution programs in schools, youth-serving organizations, or community and juvenile justice settings, most successful programs begin with an extensive needs assessment and planning process. This chapter will use the school setting as an example of developing and implementing a conflict resolution education program, but this information is transferable to settings in youth-serving organizations, community programs, and juvenile justice facilities.

To develop, implement, and sustain a successful conflict resolution program, participants must embrace the belief that conflicts can be resolved peacefully. Many adults in schools and other youth-serving settings are familiar with and most comfortable using conflict resolution that is grounded in methods such as the exercise of adult authority, reliance on school rules, discipline hearings, and other administrative procedures. Moving from these methods to one that encourages people to talk about their interests and needs and to work collaboratively to come up with solutions requires a major paradigm shift.

It is important to realize that students' success in developing an awareness of the positive potential of conflict resolution is an outgrowth of the endeavors and commitment exhibited by the adults in the school to approach conflict in a positive way. Educators who bring positive ways of resolving conflict into their classrooms will see results that will have a powerful effect on their own lives and work as well as on the lives and work of their students and on the communities in which they live.

A successful conflict resolution education program is the product of a continuous process that begins by organizing a planning team with broad representation

> Many minor arguments become deadly confrontations because many young people only know how to use violence to solve their problems. Conflict resolution education shows them another way.
>
> *Attorney General Janet Reno[1]*

of the school community, including parents, teachers, administrators, and community representatives. Many schools will be able to use the school advisory committees or site-based councils that are already in place as a planning team. The planning team is responsible for conducting a needs assessment and for facilitating the process of planning the implementation of the program. An example of a process for planning is provided in appendix H.

Analyzing School Conflict: Needs Assessment

A needs assessment is critical to establishing a conflict resolution education program that moves beyond the efforts of individual staff toward a united effort of the entire school community. The assessment surveys teachers, students, parents, and administrators to determine the nature of conflict in the school and how conflict is addressed. Support for the introduction of any new program into a school depends to a large extent on:

♦ The degree to which the school staff see that the program addresses current needs.

♦ The degree to which the program is incorporated into existing school improvement plans and extends or embellishes the school mission.

Figure 7 presents a sample of a needs assessment questionnaire. These questions are intended to help the planning team think about the kind of information needed to develop an action plan for establishing a conflict resolution program. A sample conflict resolution survey is presented in figure 8. A needs assessment form is provided in appendix E.

Selecting Conflict Resolution Education Programs/Curriculums

Once the goals and desired outcomes are clearly identified, the planning team is ready to explore various programs and curriculums that could be implemented to achieve the outcomes. Many program and curriculum resources are available (see appendix B for a representative list). A form to help school personnel determine whether a conflict resolution program or curriculum meets the criteria set forth in this *Guide* and how well it matches the needs and resources of the school is provided in appendix F. Specifically, the form facilitates assessment of:

◆ The extent to which the concept of conflict resolution is advanced.

◆ The extent to which the foundation abilities for conflict resolution are developed.

◆ The extent to which the fundamental principles of conflict resolution are incorporated into the curriculum.

◆ The extent to which problem-solving strategies are used and modeled by adults.

◆ The kinds of learning strategies that deliver the conflict resolution program to students.

◆ The various implementation components of conflict resolution.

In addition to a written assessment, it may be helpful to talk with individuals who have used the programs and curriculums being considered. Asking questions about what has worked, what has not worked, and why can provide information that will focus the selection process. Also, materials should be previewed to be sure that they are age appropriate.

Often schools combine various curriculums or portions of curriculums to create their own programs.

Implementing Conflict Resolution Education

There are many ways to introduce conflict resolution education. Students tend to learn to resolve conflicts best through experiential learning activities incorporated into specific curriculum areas (English or social studies, for example) and through seeing adults model conflict resolution successfully. An individual classroom teacher can provide conflict resolution training for the students of that classroom through a process curriculum or a peaceable classroom approach. Several staff can develop and implement a schoolwide peer mediation program. All staff members can agree to implement one of the problem-solving strategies of conflict resolution—perhaps negotiation or consensus decisionmaking—in every classroom of the school. The entire school community can decide to commit to the long-term development of a peaceable school, with the commitment eventually reaching beyond the school to the creation of peaceable homes and a peaceable community.

A high school can decide that all ninth grade students will be taught conflict resolution skills over a 10-week period. English teachers can integrate conflict resolution into their curriculum during one class per week and then expand the weekly lesson into their other lessons during the week. School counselors and administrators often co-teach with the classroom teacher to provide mutual support for the teaching of conflict resolution skills and strategies.

Selecting Staff Development Providers/Trainers

Regardless of which program or curriculum is chosen, it is important to select staff development providers carefully. Quality trainers are experienced in resolving conflicts in schools and in implementing programs in schools. The forms in appendix G can help school personnel to assess the offerings and

Figure 7: Sample Needs Assessment Questionnaire

- To what extent are conflicts interfering with teaching and learning processes within the school?

- What percentage of conflicts is attributable to:
  - The competitive atmosphere of the school or classroom?
  - An intolerant atmosphere in the school or classroom?
  - Poor communication?
  - Inappropriate expression of emotion?
  - Lack of conflict resolution skills?
  - Adult misuse of authority in the school or classroom?

- To what extent are diversity issues manifested as conflicts in the school community?

- To what extent is representation in decisionmaking an issue manifested in the conflicts observed in the school?

- What percentage of the conflicts arising in the school is:
  - Between students?
  - Between teachers and students?
  - Between teachers?
  - Between students and school expectations, rules, or policies?
  - Between teachers and administrators?
  - Between school staff and parents?
  - Between other groups specific to the school?

- What procedures are followed when conflicts cause disruption of teaching and learning processes? Who administers which procedures?

- Who are the sources of referrals to these procedures?

- How effective are these procedures according to the perceptions of students? parents? teachers? administrators? others?

- What existing attitudes or behavior will facilitate the implementation of a conflict resolution program in the school? Who exhibits these?

- What existing attitudes or behavior will impede the implementation of a conflict resolution program in the school? Who exhibits these?

- Which foundation skills for conflict resolution are now included in the school curriculum? When are they developed? Who provides the training in these skills? Which students receive this training?

- Which staff members have training in conflict resolution? How many hours of training?

- What staff development opportunities in conflict resolution are available? What opportunities are desired?

- What present and future monetary resources are available to support implementation of a conflict resolution program?

- What conflict resolution processes currently exist within the school? Within the school community?

- What community resources exist to assist the school in designing and implementing a conflict resolution program?

Figure 8: Sample Conflict Resolution Survey

Respond to the following statements by circling the number you believe to be most accurate.

1	2	3	4	5
Strongly Disagree				Strongly Agree

1. There are conflicts interfering with the educational process within the school.

   1   2   3   4   5

2. There is an atmosphere of intolerance within the school.

   1   2   3   4   5

3. There is a lack of a process for dealing with conflicts within the school.

   1   2   3   4   5

4. Student-student conflicts are a problem within the school.

   1   2   3   4   5

5. Student-teacher conflicts are a problem within the school.

   1   2   3   4   5

6. Teacher-teacher conflicts are a problem within the school.

   1   2   3   4   5

7. The school does not have adequate procedures for handling conflicts within the school.

   1   2   3   4   5

8. Current procedures for conflict resolution are effective.

   1   2   3   4   5

9. The school would benefit from a conflict resolution program.

   1   2   3   4   5

10. Additional Comments:

---

competency of providers of conflict resolution training and to determine how well they meet the training needs the school has identified. Before contracting the services of a staff development provider, a school should interview the provider and contact references to obtain information on the provider's performance in various school settings. Clearly, quality staff development programs include ways to build the capacity of the school to do its own training in the future.

Important Factors for Successful Implementation

Both research findings and practitioner experience support the idea that tailoring a program to a given site strengthens the probability of its success. Programs that are designed to address specific concerns, use existing resources, and build the capacity of staff are more likely to be sustained over time.

Pitfalls To Avoid

Going Too Fast

Eagerness to implement a program can lead to beginning without adequate discussion and preparation. Successful programs develop from careful planning and training before implementation is begun. Programs implemented without adequate preparation tend to be less successful and to hinder the implementation of future programs. People say, "We tried that one time but it didn't work, so let's not try now."

Going Without Support

Programs usually fail when administrators and faculty have no knowledge of or do not support "interest-based" conflict resolution approaches. Administrators and faculty who feel no responsibility for achieving the program's goals will not help support the program.

Selecting the Wrong Program and Trainers

Failure to match the program to the school's particular needs will result in problems. Successful implementation of a program at one school does not mean it will be the right program for every school. Selecting a trainer who is not qualified or who will not build the school's training capacity will also create future problems in implementing and, more importantly, in sustaining a program.

Failing To "Hang In There" for the Long Haul

Abandoning a program when it gets difficult or seems to be in a logjam is a mistake. With so many other demands on teachers, counselors, and administrators, it is tempting to stop some of the more time-consuming activities that are not specifically academic in nature. However, true results from conflict resolution programs are seen only after some time has elapsed.

Laura Otey, Administrator, K–12
Austin Independent School District, Austin, Texas[2]

However, the commitment and support of the administration, faculty, and parents appear to be universal success factors for conflict resolution education programs.

Administrative Commitment and Support

Every successful conflict resolution education program enjoys leadership and support from both the school's and the school district's administration. Administrators provide leadership and support for programs in a variety of ways:

◆ Using staff meetings and parent meetings to discuss programs and their benefits in relation to student/adult outcomes.

◆ Participating in training and staff development programs.

◆ Leading staff meetings and problem-solving sessions using conflict resolution processes.

◆ Recognizing program success during assemblies, schoolwide announcements, parent-teacher association meetings, school board meetings, and on other occasions.

◆ Making use of effective conflict management and the language of conflict resolution in the school and on the playground.

◆ Teaching or co-teaching conflict resolution lessons in the classroom.

Faculty Commitment and Support

When the faculty have little knowledge of the principles and the processes of conflict resolution, a conflict resolution program is not likely to be sustained. If faculty are not involved in training and program development, they are not likely to accept responsibility for achieving the program's goals. Behind every successful program is a core of faculty who believe passionately in the value of having students and adults resolve their differences through conflict resolution processes. These people are typically the driving force of the program through their enthusiasm, problem-solving skills, support for others in trying something new, and refusal to give up.

Successful programs involve the faculty in program planning and give them adequate initial and ongoing training. Programs implemented without adequate planning and training are not usually sustainable. A shared vision among faculty is a fundamental building block of program success. One way to ensure faculty commitment is to involve them in program development through a strategic planning process. Appendix H provides a brief description of the essential components of a strategic plan.

Parent Involvement and Support

Parents, like administrators and faculty, need to understand the programs that are being implemented in their children's school. Their support is important to the success of those programs and can be built through presentations at parent meetings in the school and in the community. Presentations in which students demonstrate the conflict resolution process provide an excellent forum for discussion. Parents can serve as volunteers helping to implement the program or can attend conflict resolution training designed especially for them. Involving parents extends conflict resolution beyond the classroom.

Program Evaluation

Any program in schools today needs to establish performance goals and to measure progress toward achieving those goals. An evaluation must show whether the program is reaching its goals (student and adult outcomes) and how it is enhancing the learning process. Program evaluation also provides valuable data for continuous improvement. Programs that are unable to report progress, outcomes, and impact rigorously are not likely to survive.

Implementing a conflict resolution program is an extremely complex process that demands considerable energy and time from the adults involved. The impact of conflict resolution programs occurs over time. It is important to remember that conflict resolution education is not a "quick fix." The initial time invested eventually pays off in time gained when students resolve their own problems without the intervention of the adults in the school.

Notes

1. Reno, J. 1996. "Attorney General Announces New Effort To Prevent School Violence." U.S. Department of Justice press release, May 29, 1996.

2. Otey, L. 1996 (May). Personal communication.

Appendix A: Contact Information

The first section of this appendix, "Conflict Resolution Consultation and Training Resources," supplies contact information for a number of organizations that provide national leadership in the field of conflict resolution education through their efforts to promote, develop, implement, and institutionalize conflict resolution education programs. This list is not intended to be comprehensive.

The second section of the appendix, "Programs Cited in This *Guide*," provides contact information for the community programs described in chapter 7. Community mediation centers are an excellent initial resource for information about local programs on conflict resolution education.

Conflict Resolution Consultation and Training Resources

American Bar Association
Section of Dispute Resolution
740 15th Street NW., Ninth Floor
Washington, DC 20005
202–662–1680
202–662–1032 (fax)

Anti-Defamation League
A World of Difference Program
823 United Nations Plaza
New York, NY 10017
212–885–7810
212–490–0187 (fax)

Children's Creative Response to Conflict
P.O. Box 271
Nyack, NY 10960
914–353–1796
914–358–4924 (fax)

Community Board Program, Inc.
Conflict Resolution Resources for Schools and Youth
1540 Market Street, Suite 490
San Francisco, CA 94102
415–552–1250
415–626–0595 (fax)

Conflict Resolution and Cooperative Learning Center
Teaching Students To Be Peacemakers Program
University of Minnesota
College of Education and Human Development
60 Peik Hall
159 Pillsbury Drive SE.
Minneapolis, MN 55455
612–624–7031
612–626–1395 (fax)

Educators for Social Responsibility
23 Garden Street
Cambridge, MA 02138
617–492–1764
617–864–5164 (fax)

Harvard Negotiation Project
500 Pound Hall
Harvard Law School
Cambridge, MA 02138
617–495–1684
617–495–7818 (fax)

Illinois Institute for Dispute Resolution
National Peaceable School Project
110 West Main Street
Urbana, IL 61801
217–384–4118
217–384–8280 (fax)

International Center for Cooperation
and Conflict Resolution
Teachers College at Columbia University
525 West 120th Street
Box 53
New York, NY 10027
212–678–3402
212–678–4048 (fax)

Iowa Peace Institute
917 10th Avenue
P.O. Box 480
Grinnell, IA 50112
515–236–4880
515–236–6905 (fax)

National Association for Community Mediation
1726 M Street NW., Suite 500
Washington, DC 20036–4502
202–467–6226
202–466–4769 (fax)

National Crime Prevention Council
1700 K Street NW., Second Floor
Washington, DC 20006–3817
202–466–6272
202–296–1356 (fax)

National Institute for Citizen Education
in the Law
711 G Street SE.
Washington, DC 20003
202–546–6644
202–546–6649 (fax)

National Institute for Dispute Resolution
National Association for Mediation in Education
1726 M Street NW., Suite 500
Washington, DC 20036–4502
202–466–4764
202–466–4769 (fax)

National School Safety Center
4165 Thousand Oaks Boulevard, Suite 290
Westlake Village, CA 91362
805–373–9977
805–373–9277 (fax)

New Mexico Center for Dispute Resolution
National Resource Center for Youth Mediation
800 Park Avenue SW.
Albuquerque, NM 87102
800–249–6884 (publications)
505–247–0571 (information)
505–242–5966 (fax)

Ohio Commission on Dispute Resolution
and Conflict Management
77 South High Street, 24th Floor
Columbus, OH 43266
614–752–9595
614–752–9682 (fax)

Peace Education Foundation
1900 Biscayne Boulevard
Miami, FL 33132
800–749–8838
305–576–5075
305–576–3106 (fax)

Program for Young Negotiators, Inc.
20 University Road
Cambridge, MA 02138
888–832–2479 [888–TEACH–PYN (toll free)]
617–354–8467 (fax)

Resolving Conflict Creatively Program
National Center
163 Third Avenue
P.O. Box 103
New York, NY 10003
212–387–0225
212–387–0510 (fax)

Programs Cited in This *Guide*

The Arts and Conflict Resolution

Arts and Prevention Projects
U.S. Department of Education
Office of Elementary and Secondary Education
Safe and Drug-Free Schools Program
1250 Maryland Avenue SW.
Washington, DC 20202–6123
202–260–3954
202–260–3748 (fax)

California Lawyers for the Arts
Northern California Program
Fort Mason Center, Building C, Room 255
San Francisco, CA 94123
415–775–7200
415–775–1143 (fax)

Southern California Program
1641 18th Street
Santa Monica, CA 90404
310–998–5590
310–998–5594 (fax)

National Assembly of Local Arts Agencies
927 15th Street NW., 12th Floor
Washington, DC 20005
202–371–2830
202–371–0424 (fax)

National Endowment for the Arts
1100 Pennsylvania Avenue NW., Room 726
Washington, DC 20506
202–682–5537
202–682–5613 (fax)

Pathways to Success Program
U.S. Department of Justice
Office of Juvenile Justice and Delinquency
   Prevention
633 Indiana Avenue NW.
Washington, DC 20531
202–307–1150
202–514–6382 (fax)

Urban smARTS
Department of Arts and Cultural Affairs
222 East Houston, Suite 500
San Antonio, TX 78205
210–222–2787
210–228–0263 (fax)

Washington Area Lawyers for the Arts
410 Eighth Street NW., Suite 601
Washington, DC 20004
202–393–2826
202–393–4444 (fax)

Community-Based Programs

AmeriCorps Conflict Resolution Training Project
National Association for Community Mediation
1726 M Street NW., Suite 500
Washington, DC 20036–4502
202–467–6226
202–466–4769 (fax)

Boys & Girls Clubs of America
National Headquarters
1230 West Peachtree Street NW.
Atlanta, GA 30309–3447
404–815–5781
404–815–5757 (fax)

Conflict Managers Program
Community Board Program, Inc.
1540 Market Street, Suite 490
San Francisco, CA 94102
415–552–1250
415–626–0595 (fax)

East Cleveland Youth Services Mobile
   Mediation Project
14801 Shaw Avenue
East Cleveland, OH 44112
216–681–7526
216–681–5733 (fax)

Effective Alternatives in Reconciliation Services
3319 Rochambeau Avenue
Bronx, NY 10467
718–654–4931
718–654–4942 (fax)

Lawyers Adopt-a-School Program
American Bar Association
Section of Dispute Resolution
740 15th Street NW., Seventh Floor
Washington, DC 20005
202–662–1687
202–662–1683 (fax)

Roxbury Conflict Resolution Project
The Conflict Management Group
20 University Road
Cambridge, MA 02138
617–354–5444
617–354–8467 (fax)

Second Step Program
Committee for Children
2203 Airport Way South, Suite 500
Seattle, WA 98134–2027
206–343–1223
206–343–1445 (fax)

Parent Education

Franklin Mediation Service
97 Franklin Street
Greenfield, MA 01301
413–774–7469
413–773–3834 (fax)

Parents Anonymous, Inc.
675 West Foothill Boulevard, Suite 220
Claremont, CA 91711
909–621–6184
909–625–6304 (fax)

Parents as Teachers National Center
10176 Corporate Square Drive, Suite 230
St. Louis, MO 63132
314–432–4330
314–432–8963 (fax)

Community Relations Service, U.S. Department of Justice

Regional Offices

Region I: New England (Connecticut, Maine, Massachusetts, New Hampshire, Rhode Island, Vermont)
99 Summer Street, Suite 1820
Boston, MA 02110
617–424–5717
617–424–5727 (fax)

Region II: Northeast (New Jersey, New York, Puerto Rico, Virgin Islands)
26 Federal Plaza, Room 3402
New York, NY 10278
212–264–0700
212–264–2143 (fax)

Region III: Mid-Atlantic (Delaware, District of Columbia, Maryland, Pennsylvania, Virginia, West Virginia)
Room 208 Custom House
Second and Chestnut Streets
Philadelphia, PA 19106
215–597–2344
215–597–9148 (fax)

Region IV: Southeast (Alabama, Florida, Georgia, Kentucky, Mississippi, North Carolina, South Carolina, Tennessee)
75 Piedmont Avenue NE., Room 900
Atlanta, GA 30303
404–331–6883
404–331–4471 (fax)

Region V: Midwest (Illinois, Indiana, Michigan, Minnesota, Ohio, Wisconsin)
55 West Monroe Street, Suite 420
Chicago, IL 60603
312–353–4391
312–353–4390 (fax)

Region VI: Southwest (Arkansas, Louisiana, New Mexico, Oklahoma, Texas)
1420 West Mockingbird Lane, Suite 250
Dallas, TX 75247
214–655–8175
214–655–8184 (fax)

Region VII: Central (Iowa, Kansas, Missouri, Nebraska)
323 West Eighth Street, Suite 301
Kansas City, MO 64105
816–374–6522
816–374–6530 (fax)

Region VIII: Rocky Mountain (Colorado, Montana, North Dakota, South Dakota, Utah, Wyoming)
1244 Speer Boulevard, Room 650
Denver, CO 80204–3584
303–844–2973
303–844–2907 (fax)

Region IX: Western (Arizona, California, Guam, Hawaii, Nevada)
33 New Montgomery Street, Suite 1840
San Francisco, CA 94105
415–744–6565
415–744–6590 (fax)

Region X: Northwest (Alaska, Idaho, Oregon, Washington)
915 Second Avenue, Room 1898
Seattle, WA 98174
206–220–6700
206–220–6706 (fax)

Field Offices

Detroit Field Office
211 West Fort Street, Suite 1404
Detroit, MI 48226
313–226–4010
313–226–2568 (fax)

Houston Field Office
515 Rusk Avenue, Room 12605
Houston, TX 77002
713–718–4861
713–718–4862 (fax)

Los Angeles Field Office
888 South Figueroa Street, Suite 1880
Los Angeles, CA 90071
213–894–2941
213–894–2880 (fax)

Miami Field Office
51 SW. First Avenue, Room 424
Miami, FL 33130
305–536–5206
305–536–7363 (fax)

Appendix B: Conflict Resolution Curriculum Resources

The intent of this appendix is to illustrate some of the most current and readily available conflict resolution curriculum resources. These representative materials were selected through a nomination process by national leaders in the field of conflict resolution education. This list is neither exhaustive nor intended as a recommendation of these curriculums by the U.S. Department of Justice or the U.S. Department of Education. The materials have been categorized into five groups: Foundation Abilities, Process Curriculum, Mediation, Peaceable Classroom, and Peaceable School.

Many of the publications listed here are available through the Office of Juvenile Justice and Delinquency Prevention's Juvenile Justice Clearinghouse, a component of the National Criminal Justice Reference Service (NCJRS). An NCJ (National Criminal Justice) number after a citation indicates that the publication is available from the Clearinghouse on microfiche or through paper reproduction or interlibrary loan. For further information, contact the Clearinghouse by telephone at 800–638–8736; via the electronic bulletin board at 301–738–8895; or through the Internet at askncjrs@ncjrs.org.

Foundation Abilities

Aggressors, Victims, & Bystanders: Thinking and Acting to Prevent Violence. 1994. Ronald Slaby, Renee Wilson-Brewer, and Kimberly Dash, Education Development Center, 55 Chapel Street, Newton, MA 02160.
Phone: 800–225–4276
Audience: Grades 6–9.
Focus: To develop skills in solving social problems nonviolently and in evaluating beliefs regarding violence.

Key Teaching Strategies: Full-class and small-group discussions, games, role-playing, and skill-building exercises.
Type of Material: Teacher's guide and handouts.
Cost: $45.

Anti-bias Curriculum: Tools for Empowering Young Children. 1989. Louise Derman-Sparks and the ABC Task Force, National Association for the Education of Young Children, 1509 16th Street NW., Washington, DC 20036–1426. **NCJ 160365.**
Phone: 202–232–8777
Audience: Ages 2–5.
Focus: To promote critical thinking regarding cultural bias and diversity and problem-solving processes to resolve conflict.
Key Teaching Strategies: Activities and discussions.
Type of Material: Teacher's guide.
Cost: $17.

Circles of Learning: Cooperation in the Classroom. 1984, 1986, 1990, 1993. David W. Johnson, Robert T. Johnson, and Edythe Holuhec, Interaction Book Company, 7208 Cornelia Drive, Edina, MN 55435.
Phone: 612–831–9500
Audience: Grades K–8.
Focus: To teach students to work cooperatively to achieve mutual learning goals. Program is research and theory based.
Key Teaching Strategies: Experiential/cooperative learning, simulations, role-playing, and perspective taking.
Type of Material: Book, videos, student manual, and audiocassettes.
Cost: Book, $10; video, $25; audiocassette, $10.

Conflict Management: Middle School Curriculum.
1990. Elizabeth Loescher, The Conflict Center,
2626 Osceola Street, Denver, CO 80212.
Phone: 303–433–4983
Audience: Grades 6–8.
Focus: To reduce levels of physical, verbal, and
emotional violence through skill building.
Key Teaching Strategies: Role-playing, interactive
lessons, self-evaluations, and small- and large-group
discussions.
Type of Material: Teacher's guide and handouts.
Cost: $20.

*Dealing With Anger: Givin' It, Takin' It, Workin'
It Out. A Violence Prevention Program for African
American Youth (female or male version).* 1991. Re-
search Press, Inc., P.O. Box 9177, Champaign, IL
61821.
Phone: 217–352–3273
Audience: African-American youth in grades 6–12
(each set is specific for males or females).
Focus: To teach students ways to express angry
feelings, accept criticism, and negotiate a solution.
Key Teaching Strategies: Videos, discussion, and
role-playing.
Type of Material: Video and discussion guide.
Cost: Each set of videos, $495; both sets, $740.

*Discover the World: Empowering Children to Value
Themselves, Others, and the Earth.* 1990. Susan
Hopkins and Jeffery Winters, New Society Publish-
ers, 4527 Springfield Avenue, Philadelphia, PA 19143.
Phone: 800–333–9093
Audience: Infants, toddlers, and grades pre-K
through 5; especially geared toward young children.
Focus: To teach respect for oneself and others.
Key Teaching Strategies: Activities and lesson plans
that include art, music, movement, and language.
Type of Material: Teacher's guide.
Cost: $14.95.

Everyone Wins! Cooperative Games and Activities.
1990. Sambhava and Josette Luvmour, New Society
Publishers, 4527 Springfield Avenue, Philadelphia,
PA 19143.
Phone: 800–333–9093
Audience: Grades pre-K through 4.
Focus: To increase self-esteem and interconnected-
ness with others through the interaction of game-
playing.

Key Teaching Strategies: Playing games.
Type of Material: Teacher's guide.
Cost: $8.95.

The Giraffe Classroom. 1990. Nancy Sokol Green,
Center for Non-Violent Communication, 3468
Meadowbrook Boulevard, Cleveland Heights, OH
44118–3660.
Phone: 216–371–1123
Audience: Grades 1–8.
Focus: To promote caring, cooperative, and safe
schools through teaching nonviolent communication
skills that empower children and others to get their
needs met in mutually satisfying ways.
Key Teaching Strategies: Cooperative pairs and
small-group work integrated into language, social
studies, art, and music.
Type of Material: Teacher's manual.
Cost: $14.

*Keeping the Peace: Practicing Cooperation and Con-
flict Resolution with Preschoolers.* 1989. Susanne
Wichert, New Society Publishers, 4527 Springfield
Avenue, Philadelphia, PA 19143.
Phone: 800–333–9093
Audience: Preschool children and adults who live
and work with preschool children.
Focus: To increase altruistic behavior, decrease ag-
gressive behavior, and enhance a greater tolerance
among children for the differences in others.
Key Teaching Strategies: Activities and games.
Type of Material: Teacher's guide.
Cost: Paperback, $12.95; hardcover, $34.95.

The Mayor at Kackal Heights. 1987. Rita Herzog
and Kathy Smith, Center for Non-Violent Communication, 3468 Meadowbrook Boulevard,
Cleveland Heights, OH 44118–3660.
Phone: 216–371–1123
Audience: Grades K–8.
Focus: To teach a nonviolent communication approach for solving school conflicts between children/
teachers/parents that includes stating one's own
position and appreciating the positions of others.
Key Teaching Strategies: Role-playing with puppets, class meetings, and other experiential learning
techniques.
Type of Material: Book, lesson plans, and resource
materials.

Cost: Book, $10; curriculum guide, $10; puppets, $40.

The PATHS Curriculum: Promoting Alternative Thinking Strategies. 1994. Carol A. Kusche and Mark T. Greenberg, Developmental Research and Programs, 130 Nickerson Street, Suite 107, Seattle, WA 98109.
Phone: 800–736–2630
Audience: Grades K–5.
Focus: To improve the social and emotional competence and behavior of children, reduce peer and classroom conflict, and improve both student thinking skills and classroom climate.
Key Teaching Strategies: Role-playing, stories, and other language arts activities; problem-solving meetings; peer discussions; cooperative learning; and artistic and other creative activities.
Type of Material: Scope and sequence instructional manual, lessons, pictures, and photographs.
Cost: PATHS basic kit, $550 (includes curriculum, instruction manual, materials, photographs, and posters).

Personal and Social Responsibility. 1988. Constance Dembrowsky, Institute for Affective Skill Development, P.O. Box 880, La Luz, NM 88337.
Phone: 800–745–0418
Audience: Grades 9–12.
Focus: To teach students to develop critical concepts and behavioral skills in the areas of self-esteem, responsibility, relating effectively, conflict resolution, problem solving, and goal setting.
Key Teaching Strategies: Experientially based, scoped, and sequenced one-semester course using role-playing, games, and small-group activities.
Type of Material: Teacher manual, student activity book, parent leader manual, parent activity book, and two videos.
Cost: Teacher manual, student activity book, parent leader manual, parent activity book, and two videos, $299; student activity book, $14.95; parent leader manual, $59.95; parent activity book, $7.95; videos, $59.95 each.

Productive Conflict Resolution. 1996. Colorado School Mediation Project, 3970 Broadway, Suite B3, Boulder, CO 80304.
Phone: 303–444–7671

Audience: Grades K–2, 2–5, 5–8, and high school.
Focus: To reduce violence and antisocial behavior; develop long-term change in students' and teachers' attitudes and behavior toward conflict, diversity, and decisionmaking; promote greater academic achievement and emotional intelligence; and promote a caring, cooperative, disciplined school environment where learning and creativity take place.
Key Teaching Strategies: Role-playing, discussion, brainstorming, journaling, and other experiential learning.
Type of Material: Curriculums for grades K–12, videos, and mediation training manuals.
Cost: Grades K–2, $20; grades 2–5, 5–8, and high school, $25; manuals, $9.95.

Saturday Institute for Manhood, Brotherhood Actualization (SIMBA) Replication Manual. 1996. Jennie C. Trotter and SIMBA Coalition Members, WSCI-C/O SIMBA Project, 3480 Greenbriar Parkway, Suite 310 B, Atlanta, GA 30331.
Phone: 404–699–6891
Audience: Ages 8–18.
Focus: To teach conflict resolution through the Saturday school program for juveniles. Manual includes program overview, curriculum on African-American history, program implementation steps, procedures, and schedules. The model is adaptable for community settings.
Key Teaching Strategies: Art, music, group discussions, drama, role-playing, photography, and video production.
Type of Material: Curriculum, training manuals, and videos.
Cost: Manual, $50; videos, $25.

Second Step: A Violence Prevention Curriculum, Grades PreK–K; Grades 1–3; Grades 4–5; Grades 6–8. 1992. Kathy Beland, Committee for Children, 172 20th Avenue, Seattle, WA 98122.
Phone: 800–634–4449
Audience: Grades pre-K through 8.
Focus: To reduce impulsive and aggressive behavior by teaching students foundational skills in empathy, impulse control, problem solving, and anger management.
Key Teaching Strategies: Stories/discussions, teacher modeling of behaviors and skills, activities, and role-playing.

Type of Material: 11- x 17-inch photo lesson cards, teacher guide, posters, film strip, puppets, and song tape.
Cost: Grades pre-K–K, $245; grades 1–3, $255; grades 4–5, $235; grades 6–8, $285.

Violence: Dealing with Anger. 1994. Thomas Crum, Centre Communication, 1800 30th Street, No. 207, Boulder, CO 80301.
Phone: 303–444–1166
Audience: Grades 4–6.
Focus: To teach new skills to replace violent reactions in problem situations through student role-playing.
Key Teaching Strategies: Role-playing interspersed with teaching exercises.
Type of Material: 25-minute video with teaching guide included.
Cost: $69.95.

Violence in the Schools: Developing Prevention Plans. 1994. Center for Civic Education, 5146 Douglas Fir Road, Calabasas, CA 91302–1467.
Phone: 800–350–4223
Audience: Grades 6–9.
Focus: To develop students' commitment to active citizenship and governance by teaching the knowledge and skills required for effective participation.
Key Teaching Strategies: Reading, directed discussions, writing, role-playing, small-group problem solving, cooperative learning techniques, and critical thinking exercises.
Type of Material: Teacher's guide, student text, and staff development training manual.
Cost: Teacher's guide, $10; student text, $5.50 ($5 each for orders of 10 or more); set comprising a teacher's guide and 30 student texts, $150.

Violence Prevention Curriculum for Adolescents. 1987. Deborah Prothrow-Stith, Education Development Center, Inc., 55 Chapel Street, Newton, MA 02160.
Phone: 617–969–7100
Audience: Grades 9–12.
Focus: To increase students' awareness of the causes and effects of violence; illustrate that violence is preventable; teach that anger is a normal part of life that can be expressed and channeled in healthy, constructive ways; and encourage students to think about alternatives to violence in conflict situations.

Key Teaching Strategies: Minilectures, facilitated class discussions, role-playing, and observation and analysis.
Type of Material: 110-page teacher's guide, student handouts, and video.
Cost: Teacher's guide, $30 ($25 each for orders of 10 or more); video rental, $60; teacher's guide and video, $150.

A World of Difference Institute: A National Education and Diversity Training Program of the Anti-Defamation League. Elementary Guide, Secondary Guide, and Youth Services and Pre-School Activity Guides. Anti-Defamation League, 823 United Nations Plaza, New York, NY 10017.
Phone: 212–490–2525
Audience: Grades preschool–12.
Focus: To promote positive self-concept while recognizing and appreciating diversity in all forms, and to raise awareness and understanding of the detrimental effects of racism, prejudice, anti-Semitism, and discrimination.
Key Teaching Strategies: Activities, discussion, role-playing, and readings.
Type of Material: Resource guides, audiovisual materials, and articles.
Cost: Elementary and secondary guides, $35; activity guide, $25. (Guides are only sold through teacher training sessions.)

A Year of SCRC: 35 Experiential Workshops for the Classroom. 1992. Kinshasha Nia Azariah, Frances Kern-Crotty, and Louise Gomer Bangel, Center for Peace Education, 103 William Howard Taft Road, Cincinnati, OH 45219. **NCJ 160380.**
Phone: 513–221–4863
Audience: Grades K–6.
Focus: To promote the attitudes of inclusion and respect for self and others and teach the skills needed for problem solving.
Key Teaching Strategies: Experiential learning activities, including games, role-playing, and group dialog.
Type of Material: Program guide and workshop manual.
Cost: Program guide, $15; workshop manual, $23.

Process Curriculum

Conflict Resolution: An Elementary School Curriculum. 1990. Gail Sadalla, Meg Holmberg, and Jim Halligan. **NCJ 138316.**

Conflict Resolution: A Secondary School Curriculum. 1987. Gail Sadalla, Meg Holmberg, and Jim Halligan. **NCJ 138329.**
Community Board Program, Inc., 1540 Market Street, Suite 490, San Francisco, CA 94102.
Phone: 415–552–1250
Audience: Grades K–7 and 7–12.
Focus: To help students become aware of their choices in conflict situations. Elementary curriculum includes more than 80 activities focusing on building effective communication and problem-solving skills. Secondary curriculum focuses on enabling students to reduce the tensions and hostilities associated with conflict.
Key Teaching Strategies: Role-playing, record-keeping, group discussions, brainstorming, demonstrations, small- and large-group work, and experiential practice of skills.
Type of Material: Classroom curriculum of more than 300 pages in a three-ring binder for easy copying of handout materials.
Cost: $44 each.

Conflict Resolution for Kindergarten through Grade 3. 1995. Linda Dunn, Pat Lewis, Lynda Hall, Eileen McAvoy, and Cynthia Pitts, Mediation Network of North Carolina, P.O. Box 241, Chapel Hill, NC 27514–0241.
Phone: 919–929–6333
Audience: Grades K–3.
Focus: To teach the basics of listening skills, "I"-messages, anger management, choice and consequences, feelings, perception, diversity, and negotiation. Includes a section on how to make conflict resolution part of regular classroom activities.
Key Teaching Strategies: Discussion/dialog, simulation games, role-playing, and interactive activities.
Type of Material: 191-page teaching curriculum, scoped and sequenced.
Cost: $20.

Conflict Resolution in the Schools: A Manual for Educators. 1996. National Institute for Dispute Resolution and the National Association for Mediation in Education, 1726 M Street NW., Suite 500, Washington, DC 20036.
Phone: 202–466–4764
Audience: Educators.
Focus: To show educators how to diagnose conflicts, handle difficult confrontations, and implement appropriate mediation and problem-solving strategies for classroom conflicts, violence, and community divisiveness.
Key Teaching Strategies: Introduces the concepts and skills of conflict resolution that can be practiced in the classroom and throughout the school community.
Type of Material: Book.
Cost: $35.

Conflict Resolution: Strategies for Collaborative Problem Solving. 1992. Ellen Raider and Susan Coleman, International Center for Cooperation and Conflict Resolution, Teacher's College, Columbia University, Box 53, New York, NY 10027.
Phone: 212–678–3402
Audience: Educators, parents, and youth leaders.
Focus: To teach adults conflict resolution skills that will enable them to work collaboratively to resolve disputes within their homes, communities, and workplaces, so that they can become role models for their children and colleagues.
Key Teaching Strategies: Experiential exercises and role-playing with audio/video feedback geared for the adult reader.
Type of Material: Participant manuals and train-the-trainer guide.
Cost: Not available for purchase without training within school system or at a teacher's college.

The Conflict Zoo. 1996. Suzin Glickman, Natalie Johnson, Gina Sirianni, and Judith Zimmer, National Institute for Citizen Education in the Law, 711 G Street SE., Washington, DC 20003.
Phone: 202–546–6644
Audience: Grades 3 and 4.

Focus: To teach students to identify words and actions that can lead to conflict, to understand the perspectives of all parties involved in a conflict, and to develop skills for conflict management.

Key Teaching Strategies: Critical thinking, problem solving, cooperative learning, role-playing, interviews, group dialog, brainstorming, and other experiential learning strategies.

Type of Material: Elementary curriculums.

Cost: Not available.

Creative Conflict Solving for Kids, Grade Four. 1991. Fran Schmidt and Alice Friedman. **NCJ 160386.**
Creative Conflict Solving for Kids, Grade Five. 1985. Fran Schmidt and Alice Friedman.
Creating Peace, Building Community, Grade Six. 1996. Judy Bachoy.
Creating Peace, Building Community, Grade Seven. 1996. Judy Bachoy.
Peace Education Foundation, 1900 Biscayne Boulevard, Miami, FL 33132–1025.

Phone: 800–749–8838

Audience: Grades 4–7.

Focus: *Creative Conflict Solving for Kids, Grade Four,* introduces the Rules for Fighting Fair and the fouls, the mediation process, empowerment skills such as peer refusal and assertive language, and ways to enhance conflict resolution skills and communication techniques. *Creative Conflict Solving for Kids, Grade Five,* focuses on students' perceptions of conflict by using news clippings and real-life conflicts and encouraging them to employ conflict resolution skills using goal-setting techniques. *Creating Peace, Building Community, Grade Six,* and *Creating Peace, Building Community, Grade Seven,* are designed to help students gain a strong sense of self-worth, values, and the ability to empathize with others as they learn conflict resolution skills. The sixth-grade materials focus on character development, cultural awareness, community building, conflict analysis, and aggression control. The seventh-grade materials address effective communication and empathy development; bully, victim, and bystander issues; self-empowerment; and applying peacemaking skills in the real world.

Key Teaching Strategies: Brainstorming, cooperative activities, problem solving, role-playing, simulation, and experiential learning.

Type of Material: Teacher's guide, student handbooks, and poster.

Cost: Complete set of materials for each title, $89.95; teacher's guide including student pages, $23.95.

Fighting Fair: Dr. Martin Luther King, Jr. For Kids, Grade Eight. 1990. Fran Schmidt and Alice Friedman. Peace Education Foundation, 1900 Biscayne Boulevard, Miami, FL 33132–1025.

Phone: 800–749–8838

Audience: Grade 8.

Focus: To teach nonviolent techniques for solving conflicts. Combines conflict resolution with the history of the civil rights movement.

Key Teaching Strategies: Brainstorming, cooperative activities, problem solving, role-playing, simulation, and experiential learning.

Type of Material: Teacher's guide, student handbooks, poster, and video.

Cost: Complete set of materials, $139.95; teacher's guide including student pages, $23.95.

Helping Kids Handle Conflict: A Guide for Those Teaching Children. 1995. National Crime Prevention Council, 1700 K Street NW., Second Floor, Washington, DC 20006. **NCJ 158977.**

Phone: 202–466–6272

Audience: Adults working with youth ages 5–12.

Focus: To provide classroom-based activities that supplement conflict management sessions and to introduce the philosophy of conflict management to a school or community.

Key Teaching Strategies: Short-term, self-contained activities for teachers of young persons.

Type of Material: Book, activities, followup activities, related children's books, worksheets, and standard letters to parents.

Cost: $24.95.

Life Negotiations: The PYN Curriculum for Middle Schools. 1996. Jared R. Curhan. Program for Young Negotiators, 20 University Road, Cambridge, MA 02138.

Phone: 888–832–2479

Audience: Grades 6–9.

Focus: To promote the use of collaboration, communication, and empathy, and foster an environment in which individuals can learn to cope with differences in a productive manner.

Key Teaching Strategies: Role-playing, case studies, games, performances, reading and writing assignments, videos, and classroom discussions.
Type of Material: Teacher's manuals, student activity books, and videos.
Cost: Not available for purchase without first attending the Program for Young Negotiators' training seminar on negotiation.

Peacemaking Skills for Little Kids, Pre K–K. 1993. Fran Schmidt and Alice Friedman.
Peacemaking Skills for Little Kids, Grade One. 1996. Doris Berkell, Karen Kotzen, and Sandy Rizzo.
Peacemaking Skills for Little Kids, Grade Two. 1996. Elyse Brunt, Alice Friedman, Fran Schmidt, and Theresa Solotoff.
Peace Scholars: Learning Through Literature, Grade Three. 1996. Diane Carlebach.
Peace Education Foundation, 1900 Biscayne Boulevard, Miami, FL 33132–1025.
Phone: 800–749–8838
Audience: Grades pre-K through 3.
Focus: *Peacemaking Skills for Little Kids, Pre K–K,* teaches listening and communication skills, explores emotions, and stresses cooperation and cultural tolerance, introducing students to the I-Care Rules and the PEF's conflict resolution model. *Peacemaking Skills for Little Kids, Grade One,* focuses on giving students a more indepth understanding of the I-Care Rules, stressing cooperative learning and reading, writing, and problem-solving skills. *Peacemaking Skills for Little Kids, Grade Two,* continues to build on the skills begun in the previous books, providing lessons and extension activities that can be incorporated into traditional academic subjects. *Peace Scholars: Learning Through Literature, Grade Three,* uses a collection of ethnically diverse stories and folk tales to enhance students' conflict resolution competency and teach cooperation, self-esteem, empathy, and other life skills.
Key Teaching Strategies: Puppetry, discussion, music, experiential learning, cooperative activities, role-playing.
Type of Material: Teacher's guide, student handbooks, poster, puppets, audiocassettes, and buttons.
Cost: Complete set of materials for each title, $119.95; teacher's guide including student pages, $23.95.

Time Out To Resolve It! A School-Based Conflict Resolution Program. 1994. Citizenship & Law-Related Education Center, 9738 Lincoln Village Drive, Sacramento, CA 95827.
Phone: 916–228–2322
Audience: Grades K–12.
Focus: To teach decisionmaking, problem-solving, and communication skills that help students resolve their own conflicts peacefully.
Key Teaching Strategies: Individual, small- and large-group work, practice, and discussions; role-playing; active, cooperative learning activities; performance-based assessment.
Type of Material: Student and adult training manuals, implementation manual, classroom lesson plans linked to middle and high school subject matter, and videotapes.
Cost: Currently available only in conjunction with training.

TRIBE: Conflict Resolution Curriculum for Middle School. 1994. Dee Edelman, Copper Coggins, Debbie Rios, and Kathryn Liss, The Mediation Center, 189 College Street, Asheville, NC 28801.
Phone: 704–251–6089
Audience: Grades 6–8.
Focus: To reduce violence and promote cooperative problem solving through win/win strategies, anger management, and communication and decision-making skills.
Key Teaching Strategies: Role-playing, cooperative learning, metaphorical activities, group dialog, and simulations.
Type of Material: Sequential curriculums for grades 6–8 and classroom poster.
Cost: Teacher manual, $20; classroom poster, $8.

Violence Intervention Curriculum for Families. 1996.
Violence Intervention Curriculum for Juveniles. 1996.
New Mexico Center for Dispute Resolution, 620 Roma NW., Suite B, Albuquerque, NM 87102.
Phone: 800–249–6884
Audience: High-risk youth ages 12–18.
Focus: To give youth strategies to control impulsive behaviors, manage personal behavior, make informed choices, and acknowledge the consequences of their own actions for themselves and for others.

Violence Intervention Curriculum for Families incorporates lessons for parents alone and for parents and youth together, based on the belief that healthy interaction between parents/adults and children is essential to improve family functioning and reinforce the skills taught. *Violence Intervention Curriculum for Juveniles* is directed to those who work with high-risk youth in schools and community, probation, detention, and correctional settings.

Key Teaching Strategies: Exercises in anger management, consequential thinking, problem solving, communication, conflict management, and negotiation skills. The curriculum reflects varied approaches that emphasize individual learning styles and also encourage participants to integrate concepts through active learning.

Type of Material: 200- to 225-page curriculum and 30-minute instructional videocassette (in color or black and white).

Cost: *Violence Intervention Curriculum for Families,* $109; *Violence Intervention Curriculum for Juveniles,* $99.

We Can Work It Out!: Problem Solving Through Mediation, Elementary Edition. 1996. Linda Barnes-Robinson, Sue Jewler, and Judith Zimmer.
We Can Work It Out!: Problem Solving Through Mediation, Secondary Edition. 1993. Suzin Glickman and Judith Zimmer.
National Teens, Crime, and the Community Program, c/o National Institute for Citizen Education in the Law, 711 G Street SE., Washington, DC 20003.

Phone: 202–546–6644

Audience: Grades 5–12.

Focus: To promote cooperation over competition while pursuing a nonadversarial method of conflict resolution. The lessons teach students to generate nonviolent options when faced with conflict; develop critical thinking, questioning, and active listening skills; analyze and solve problems; find common ground when they disagree; and manage conflict in their daily lives. Lessons culminate in a mock mediation where students role-play the parts of disputants and mediators and are evaluated by members of the community involved in related fields.

Key Teaching Strategies: Critical thinking, problem solving, cooperative learning, role-playing, interviews, group dialog, brainstorming, and other experiential learning strategies.

Type of Material: Curriculums for grades 5–7 (elementary edition) and 7–12 (secondary edition).

Cost: Elementary edition, $40; secondary edition, $40.

Winning Against Violent Environments (W.A.V.E.) Program. Cleveland Public Schools Center for Conflict Resolution, 1651 East 71st Street, Cleveland, OH 44103.

Phone: 216–432–4605

Audience: Students grades K–12, staff, and families.

Focus: To teach young people to create peaceful and healthy environments in which to live through problem solving, respect for cultural diversity, and communication.

Key Teaching Strategies: Experiential and cooperative learning activities, group interaction, team-building activities, and role-playing.

Type of Material: Student training, handbooks, handouts, organizational development, classroom management, curriculum infusion, and other resource materials.

Cost: $75 per student for training and all materials. Materials are available only with the training.

WinWin! 1994. Fran Schmidt. Peace Education Foundation, 1900 Biscayne Boulevard, Miami, FL 33132–1025.

Phone: 800–749–8838

Audience: Grades 9–12.

Focus: To tackle tough problems like violence, anger, cultural differences, and sexual harassment while teaching conflict resolution skills. Presented in a magazine format.

Key Teaching Strategies: Brainstorming, cooperative activities, problem solving, role-playing, simulation, reading, and experiential learning.

Type of Material: Teacher's guide, student handbooks (magazine format), poster, and video.

Cost: Complete set, $214.95.

Mediation

Arizona Department of Education Peer Mediation Video. 1992.
On-Going Training Activities for Student Mediators. 1990, revised 1995.
School Mediation Project, Our Town Family Center, P.O. Box 26665, Tucson, AZ 85726.
Phone: 520–323–1708
Audience: Student mediators, grades 3–12.
Focus: To review, sharpen, and extend student mediators' skills.
Key Teaching Strategies: Role-playing, brainstorming, group dialog, games, and worksheets.
Type of Material: Instructor's manual and orientation videos for elementary, middle, and high school.
Cost: Manual, $20.50; video, $28.

Classroom Conflict Resolution Training for Grades 3–6. 1995. Community Board Program, Inc., 1540 Market Street, Suite 490, San Francisco, CA 94102.
Phone: 415–552–1250
Audience: Grades 3–6.
Focus: To introduce conflict management concepts and skills to third through sixth grade classes before a selected group of students is trained as Conflict Managers.
Key Teaching Strategies: Activities to build communication and problem-solving skills.
Type of Material: Manual.
Cost: $13.

Conflict Management for Juvenile Treatment Facilities: A Manual for Training and Program Implementation. 1992. Meg Holmberg and Jim Halligan. Community Board Program, Inc., 1540 Market Street, Suite 490, San Francisco, CA 94102.
NCJ 138326.
Phone: 415–552–1250
Audience: Juvenile justice facility professionals.
Focus: To provide a complete overview of a program to reduce conflict and tension in juvenile treatment facilities through conflict resolution. Includes a full curriculum for training juvenile facility residents as conflict managers and also covers staff development and program evaluation.
Key Teaching Strategies: Role-playing, small-group discussion, journal keeping, cooperative games, experiential practice of skills, recordkeeping, simulations, and demonstrations.

Type of Material: Training manual and implementation guide.
Cost: $27.

Conflict Manager Training for Elementary School Students. 1995. Nancy Kaplan.
Mediation Training for Middle School Students. 1995. Nancy Kaplan.
Mediation Training for High School Students. 1995. Nancy Kaplan.
Conflict Resolution Unlimited, 845 106th Avenue NE., Suite 109, Bellevue, WA 98004.
Phone: 206–451–4015
Audience: Grades K–6, 6–9, and 9–12.
Focus: To create a comprehensive conflict resolution program for the entire school and parent community.
Key Teaching Strategies: Demonstrations, exercises, and role-playing.
Type of Material: Curriculum manual, video and leader's guide, classroom teacher's manual, and training aids. Videos and student handouts also available in Spanish.
Cost: Elementary edition: curriculum manual, $200; classroom teacher's manual, $150; video and leader's guide, $95; package consisting of all manuals, video, and teaching aids, $295. Middle school and high school editions: curriculum manual, $250; classroom teacher's manual, $200; video and leader's guide, $150; package consisting of all manuals, video, and teaching aids, $395.

Conflict Managers in Action. 1987. Community Board Program, Inc., 1540 Market Street, Suite 490, San Francisco, CA 94102.
Phone: 415–552–1250
Audience: Grades 3–12.
Focus: To introduce the program. Student conflict managers in action are highlighted, and national TV coverage of these programs in elementary, middle, and high schools is featured.
Key Teaching Strategies: Models and profiles effective peer mediation programming.
Type of Material: Video.
Cost: $30.

Conflict Managers Training Manual for Grades 3–6.
1995. Community Board Program, Inc., 1540 Market Street, Suite 490, San Francisco, CA 94102.
Phone: 415–552–1250
Audience: Grades 3–6.
Focus: To foster enhanced cooperation and reduce violence through peer mediation, effective communication, and peaceful problem-solving skills and processes.
Key Teaching Strategies: Role-playing, group discussion, experiential practice of skills, record-keeping, and demonstrations.
Type of Material: Training and implementation manual.
Cost: $17.

Conflict Resolution and Peer Mediation for Grades 4 & 5. 1995. Linda Dunn, Pat Lewis, Lynda Hall, Eileen McAvoy, and Cynthia Pitts, Mediation Network of North Carolina, P.O. Box 241, Chapel Hill, NC 27514–0241.
Phone: 919–929–6333
Audience: Grades 4 and 5.
Focus: To introduce students to the mediation process and teach the skills needed to mediate. Mediation skills are reviewed and refined in the fifth grade. Can be used to train student mediators in an individual class or for a schoolwide mediation program.
Key Teaching Strategies: Discussion/dialog, simulation games, role-playing, and interactive and experiential activities.
Type of Material: 135-page scoped and sequenced curriculum.
Cost: $20.

Establishing a Viable and Durable Peer Mediation Program—From "A" to "Z." 1995. Louis A. Siegal and Lorraine M. López, The Institute for Violence Prevention, Inc., 155 Landor Drive, Athens, GA 30606.
Phone: 706–548–4932
Audience: Grades 4–12.
Focus: To establish peer mediation programs; logistics, goals, mediator and adviser selection, training, publicity, and evaluation.
Key Teaching Strategies: Brainstorming, vocabulary games, simulation exercises, role-playing, team-building, theory, and mediation practicum.

Type of Material: Program coordinator's manual and training guide, including sample forms, overheads, and list of resources.
Cost: All materials, $199.

Fuss Busters Teacher's Guide: For Elementary School Peer Mediation. 1994. Barbara A. Davis and Paul Godfrey, The Mediation Center, 189 College Street, Asheville, NC 28801. **NCJ 160364.**
Phone: 704–251–6089
Audience: Grades 3–6.
Focus: To improve students' and teachers' communication and conflict resolution skills through a series of experiential activities and discussion.
Key Teaching Strategies: Interactive group and paired activities, role-playing, simulations, and experiential learning games.
Type of Material: Teacher's manual with lesson plans, ABC's of mediation poster.
Cost: Student manual, $18; three-color poster, $8.

Implementing Mediation in Youth Corrections Settings. 1992. Jean Sidwell and Melinda Smith, New Mexico Center for Dispute Resolution, 620 Roma NW., Suite B, Albuquerque, NM 87102. **NCJ 156847.**
Phone: 800–249–6884
Audience: Grades 6–12.
Focus: To implement the mediation process in youth corrections settings and a training curriculum to train staff and youth mediators.
Key Teaching Strategies: Small- and large-group cooperative activities, brainstorming, role-playing, and other experiential learning activities.
Type of Material: Implementation guide and mediation training curriculum.
Cost: $35.

Implementing Parent-Child Mediation in Youth Corrections Settings. 1989. Jean Sidwell and Melinda Smith, New Mexico Center for Dispute Resolution, 620 Roma NW., Suite B, Albuquerque, NM 87102. **NCJ 156847.**
Phone: 800–249–6884
Audience: Grades 6–12.
Focus: To implement parent-child mediation for families of youth returning from correctional or residential settings. Includes a curriculum to train parent-child mediators.

Key Teaching Strategies: Small- and large-group activities and experiential learning strategies.
Type of Material: Implementation guide and mediation training curriculum.
Cost: $35.

Lesson Plans for Peer Mediation Training. 1995. Daniel Joyoe, Etta Smith, and Jo Ezzo, Cleveland Mediation Center, 3000 Bridge Avenue, Cleveland, OH 44113.
Phone: 216–771–7297
Audience: Grades K–12.
Focus: To teach communication skills, especially "listening" and mediation skills.
Key Teaching Strategies: Games, exercises in awareness of self and others, and small-group role-playing.
Type of Material: Detailed lesson plans, including materials, objectives, and time needed.
Cost: $150 per set. Not available for purchase without training within the school system.

Lessons in Conflict Resolution for Grades 4–6. 1994. New Mexico Center for Dispute Resolution, 620 Roma NW., Suite B, Albuquerque, NM 87102.
Phone: 800–249–6884
Audience: Grades 4–6.
Focus: To develop an understanding of conflict, styles of conflict, feelings, anger management, communication skills, and problem solving.
Key Teaching Strategies: Small- and large-group cooperative activities, brainstorming, role-playing, personal reflection, and other experiential learning strategies.
Type of Material: Booklet.
Cost: $20.

Managing Conflict: A Curriculum for Adolescents. 1989. Noreen Duffy Copeland and Melinda Smith (editors). New Mexico Center for Dispute Resolution, 620 Roma NW., Suite B, Albuquerque, NM 87102.
Phone: 800–249–6884
Audience: Grades 7–12.
Focus: To teach communication, problem-solving, and anger management skills to youth in residential or correctional settings. This is the first in a series of three publications designed to implement mediation and conflict resolution for youth involved in the juvenile justice and corrections systems.

Key Teaching Strategies: Role-playing, self-reflection, small- and large-group activities, and some written exercises.
Type of Material: Fifteen-lesson curriculum with student handouts.
Cost: $35.00

Mediation and Conflict Resolution for Gang-Involved Youth. 1992. Sara Keeney, Jean Sidwell, and Melinda Smith, New Mexico Center for Dispute Resolution, 620 Roma NW., Suite B, Albuquerque, NM 87102. **NCJ 141474.**
Phone: 800–249–6884
Audience: Grades 6–12.
Focus: To provide training for those working with gang-involved youth. Contains mediation training activities, lessons in conflict resolution for youth, and recommendations for conducting multiparty youth mediation.
Key Teaching Strategies: Small- and large-group activities, role-playing, and other experiential learning strategies.
Type of Material: Standard school materials.
Cost: $35.

Mediation for Kids. 1992. Fran Schmidt, Alice Friedman, and Jean Marvel, Peace Education Foundation, 1900 Biscayne Boulevard, Miami, FL 33132–1025. **NCJ 160389.**
Phone: 800–749–8838
Audience: Grades 4–7.
Focus: To improve communication skills and understand the causes of conflict as students learn the mediation process.
Key Teaching Strategies: Role-playing, discussion, and cooperative activities.
Type of Material: Teacher's guide, student handbooks, and posters.
Cost: Complete set, $74.95; teacher's guide including student pages, $23.95.

Mediation: Getting to Win/Win! 1994. Fran Schmidt and James Burke, Peace Education Foundation, 1900 Biscayne Boulevard, Miami, FL 33132–1025. **NCJ 160387.**
Phone: 800–749–8838
Audience: Grades 8–12.

Focus: To teach the mediation process and advanced mediation techniques such as caucusing. Video contains a demonstration of each step of the mediation process.

Key Teaching Strategies: Role-playing, discussion, reading, video, and cooperative activities.

Type of Material: Teacher's guide, student handbooks, posters, and video.

Cost: Complete set, $159.95; teacher's guide including student pages, $29.95.

Peace by Peace. 1995. The Bureau for At-Risk Youth, 645 New York Avenue, P.O. Box 670, Huntington, NY 11743. **NCJ 160362.**

Phone: 516–673–4584

Audience: Grades 6–12.

Focus: To teach students how to resolve student disputes by communicating, negotiating, and showing mutual respect.

Key Teaching Strategies: Guided discovery techniques, role-playing, and group discussion.

Type of Material: Student workbook and facilitator's guide.

Cost: Complete program, $179.95.

Peer Mediation: Conflict Resolution in Schools. 1996. Revised edition. Fred Schrumpf, Donna Crawford, and Richard Bodine, Research Press, Inc., P.O. Box 9177, Champaign, IL 61826. **NCJ 160449.**

Phone: 217–352–3273

Audience: Grades 6–12.

Focus: To develop a peer-based mediation program for faculty, student body, and peer mediators through basic and advanced training and through strategic program implementation guidelines.

Key Teaching Strategies: Experiential learning activities, simulations, group discussions, and schedule options for training.

Type of Material: Program guide with forms, student manual, and video.

Cost: Program guide, $25.95; student manual, $10.95; video, program guide, and student manual, $365; video rental, $55.

Peer Mediation Manual for Middle Schools and High Schools. 1995. Cynthia Joyce, Community Mediation, Inc., 134 Grand Avenue, New Haven, CT 06513.

Phone: 203–782–3500

Audience: Grades 5–12.

Focus: To implement peer mediation training and school-based peer mediation programs.

Key Teaching Strategies: Interactive training for extracurricular peer mediation program.

Type of Material: Manual includes exercises, games, and role-playing.

Cost: $45.

Peer Mediator Training Manual for Elementary School Students. 1995. Cheryl Cutrona, Devonne Coleman-White, Mary Beth Flynn, Anna Beale, Bob Napper, and Troy Martin, Good Shepherd Mediation Program, 5356 Chew Avenue, Philadelphia, PA 19138.

Phone: 215–843–5413

Audience: Grades 4 and 5.

Focus: To offer students training in peer mediation and an understanding of the role that conflict plays in their own lives.

Key Teaching Strategies: Brainstorming, cooperative games, role-playing, group dialog, and team-building exercises.

Type of Material: Training manual, handouts, and interactive exercises.

Cost: Manual, handouts, and exercises, $20.

Resolving Conflict: Activities for Grades K–3. 1989. Noreen Copeland and Faith Garfield, New Mexico Center for Dispute Resolution, 620 Roma NW., Suite B, Albuquerque, NM 87102.

Phone: 800–249–6884

Audience: Grades K–3.

Focus: To integrate the teaching of communication and conflict resolution skills into language arts or social studies curriculums.

Key Teaching Strategies: Role-playing, group dialog, brainstorming, learning centers, affective art activities, and other experiential learning strategies.

Type of Material: Booklet.

Cost: $15.

Starting a Conflict Manager Program. 1992. Community Board Program, Inc., 1540 Market Street, Suite 490, San Francisco, CA 94102.

Phone: 415–552–1250

Audience: Grades 3–12.

Focus: To provide a complete overview of implementing the Conflict Manager program in elementary, middle, or high schools.

Key Teaching Strategies: Five-step implementation process to secure support, train teachers, plan implementation, train students, and maintain a successful program.
Type of Material: Manual.
Cost: $25.

Student Mediator Manual for Middle and High Schools. 1995. Pat Lewis, Eileen McAvoy, Pamela Sherman, and Shelvia Whitehurst. Mediation Network of North Carolina, P.O. Box 241, Chapel Hill, NC 27514–0241.
Phone: 919–929–6333
Audience: Student mediators in middle and high school.
Focus: To serve as a guide for student mediators during training and as a reference after they become practitioners. Topics include mediator responsibilities, confidentiality, stages of mediation, preparing for the mediation session, staying in control of the mediation, a checklist for a good resolution, and samples of helpful forms.
Key Teaching Strategies: Practice exercises to develop reflective and active listening skills and communication skills; reminder forms.
Type of Material: Manual (32 pages, soft-cover, spiral-bound).
Cost: $7.

Students Resolving Conflict: Peer Mediation in Schools. 1995. Richard Cohen, GoodYear Books, Scott Foresman and Company, 1900 East Lake Avenue, Glenview, IL 60025. **NCJ 160061.**
Phone: 617–876–6074
Audience: Grades 6–12.
Focus: To guide educators in implementing peer mediation programs in their schools. Theory and practice of mediation, including overview of conflict resolution and mediation theory, technical assistance for implementing a program, conflict resolution lessons for delivery to all students, program forms, and mediation transcripts.
Key Teaching Strategies: Role-playing, discussion, brainstorming, games, worksheets, and group dialog.
Type of Material: Text.
Cost: $14.95.

Training and Implementation Guide for Student Mediation in Elementary Schools. 1990. Sara Keeney and Jean Sidwell. **NCJ 160378.**
Training and Implementation Guide for Student Mediation in Secondary Schools. 1990. Melinda Smith and Jean Sidwell. **NCJ 160379.**
New Mexico Center for Dispute Resolution, 620 Roma NW., Suite B, Albuquerque, NM 87102.
Phone: 800–249–6884
Audience: Grades K–5 and 6–12.
Focus: To prepare school staff to implement a schoolwide mediation program.
Key Teaching Strategies: Small- and large-group activities, brainstorming, and other experiential learning strategies.
Type of Material: Step-by-step staff implementation guide and mediation training curriculum.
Cost: $35.

Training Middle School Conflict Managers. 1996.
Training High School Conflict Managers. 1996.
Community Board Program, Inc., 1540 Market Street, Suite 490, San Francisco, CA 94102.
Phone: 415–552–1250
Audience: Grades 6–9 and 9–12.
Focus: To prepare high school students to be conflict managers who will help their peers resolve disputes peacefully.
Key Teaching Strategies: Role-playing, simulations, group discussion, experiential practice of skills, and recordkeeping.
Type of Material: Training and implementation manual.
Cost: $17.

Peaceable Classroom

Conflict Resolution in the Middle School. 1994. William Kreidler, Educators for Social Responsibility, 23 Garden Street, Cambridge, MA 02138.
Phone: 617–492–1764
Audience: Grades 6–8.
Focus: To teach conflict resolution skills.
Key Teaching Strategies: Role-playing, writing a journal, minilectures, brainstorming, microlabs, and small-group discussion.

Type of Material: Curriculum and teaching guide, and student handouts.
Cost: $35.

Creative Conflict Resolution: More than 200 Activities for Keeping Peace in the Classroom. 1984. William J. Kreidler, GoodYear Books, Scott Foresman and Company, 1900 East Lake Avenue, Glenview, IL 60025. **NCJ 160369.**
Phone: 800–628–4480
Audience: Grades K–6.
Focus: To teach conflict resolution techniques.
Key Teaching Strategies: Discussion, example, activity, and worksheet.
Type of Material: Resource and workbook.
Cost: $12.95.

Creative Controversy: Intellectual Challenge in the Classroom. 1987, 1992, 1995. David W. Johnson and Roger T. Johnson, Interaction Book Company, 7208 Cornelia Drive, Edina, MN 55435.
Phone: 612–831–9500
Audience: Grades K–12 and adults.
Focus: To increase students' motivation to learn, academic achievement, creative thinking, and higher level reasoning. Students research a position, present it persuasively, try to refute the opposing position, and synthesize the two positions into their "best reasoned judgment."
Key Teaching Strategies: Experiential/cooperative learning, simulations, role-playing, and perspective taking.
Type of Material: Book, video, and audiocassette.
Cost: Book, $25; video, $25; audiocassette, $10.

Elementary Perspectives: Teaching Concepts of Peace and Conflict. 1990. William J. Kreidler, Educators for Social Responsibility, 23 Garden Street, Cambridge, MA 02138. **NCJ 160426.**
Phone: 800–370–2515
Audience: K–6 educators.
Focus: To help students acquire the concrete cooperative and conflict resolution skills needed to become caring and socially responsible citizens. Contains more than 80 activities designed to help teachers and students define peace, explore justice, and learn the value of conflict and its resolution.
Key Teaching Strategies: Role-playing, songs, writing, discussions, and cooperative activities.

Type of Material: Curriculum.
Cost: $28.

The Friendly Classroom for a Small Planet: A Handbook on Creative Approaches to Living and Problem Solving for Children. 1988. Priscilla Prutzman, Lee Stern, M. Lenard Burger, and Gretchen Bodenhamer, Children's Creative Response to Conflict, P.O. Box 271, Nyack, NY 10960. **NCJ 160383.**
Phone: 914–353–1796
Audience: Grades pre-K through 6.
Focus: To teach conflict resolution skills to those who work with young people.
Key Teaching Strategies: Experiential activities, including role-playing and small-group work.
Type of Material: Handbook.
Cost: $14.95.

Making Choices about Conflict, Security, and Peace-making—Part I: Personal Perspectives. 1994. Carol Miller-Lieber, Educators for Social Responsibility, 23 Garden Street, Cambridge, MA 02138. **NCJ 160430.**
Phone: 800–370–2515
Audience: Grades 9–12.
Focus: To explore with high school students the nature of conflict and its relation to public policy; to build a "conflict toolbox" to help students resolve their conflicts without resorting to violence; and to provide practical classroom management tools.
Key Teaching Strategies: Hands-on activities, role-playing, group brainstorming, innovative projects, and problem-solving activities.
Type of Material: Curriculum.
Cost: $25.

Peacemaking Made Practical: A Conflict Management Curriculum for the Elementary School. 1991. Elizabeth Loescher, The Conflict Center, 2626 Osceola Street, Denver, CO 80212.
Phone: 303–433–4983
Audience: Grades pre-K through 6.
Focus: To reduce levels of physical, verbal, and emotional violence by raising students' awareness of conflict in our lives and teaching practical ways to make it productive.
Key Teaching Strategies: Modified lecture, group discussions, role-playing, written exercises, and games.

Type of Material: Teacher's guide.
Cost: $25.

Talk It Out: Conflict Resolution for the Elementary Teacher. 1996. Barbara Porro, Association for Supervision and Curriculum Development, 1250 North Pitt Street, Alexandria, VA 22314.
Phone: 703–549–9110
Audience: Elementary teachers.
Focus: To incorporate conflict resolution training into a daily program at the moment when students disagree.
Key Teaching Strategies: Uses 54 children's problems to teach them the skills of managing anger, listening, oral communication, and critical thinking.
Type of Material: Book.
Cost: $18.95.

Teaching Students To Be Peacemakers. 1987, 1991, 1995. David W. Johnson and Roger T. Johnson, Interaction Book Company, 7208 Cornelia Drive, Edina, MN 55435. **NCJ 160422.**
Phone: 612–831–9500
Audience: Grades K–12 and adults.
Focus: To create a cooperative learning community, teach all students how to negotiate and mediate, rotate the responsibility of mediator so that all students have their turn, and continue to teach students negotiation and mediation skills throughout the school year. Research base is presented.
Key Teaching Strategies: Experiential/cooperative learning, simulations, role-playing, and perspective taking.
Type of Material: Book, student manuals, video, and audiocassettes.
Cost: Book, $25; video, $25; audiocassettes, $10.

Teaching Young Children in Violent Times. 1994. Diane Levin, Educators for Social Responsibility, 23 Garden Street, Cambridge, MA 02138.
Phone: 800–370–2515
Audience: Grades pre-K through 3.
Focus: To teach young children to develop the understanding and skills for living peacefully with others.
Key Teaching Strategies: Teacher-led discussions, role-playing, class games, and rituals.
Type of Material: Teacher's guide.
Cost: $16.95.

Peaceable School

Creating the Peaceable School: A Comprehensive Program for Teaching Conflict Resolution. 1994. Richard Bodine, Donna Crawford, and Fred Schrumpf, Research Press, Inc., P.O. Box 9177, Champaign, IL 61826. **NCJ 154760.**
Phone: 217–352–3273
Audience: Grades 3–12.
Focus: To create a cooperative school environment through the institution of a rights and responsibilities approach to discipline where both adults and students learn to manage and resolve conflicts using the strategies of negotiation, mediation, and group problem solving.
Key Teaching Strategies: Experiential learning activities, learning centers, cooperative learning, simulations, and class meetings.
Type of Material: Program guide, student manual, and video.
Cost: Program guide, $35.95; student manual, $14.95; video, program guide, and student manual, $365; video rental, $55.

Resolving Conflict Creatively: A Teaching Guide for Grades Kindergarten Through Six. 1993. **NCJ 160361.**
Resolving Conflict Creatively: A Teaching Guide for Secondary Schools. 1990.
RCCP National Center, 163 Third Avenue, No. 103, New York, NY 10003.
Phone: 212–387–0225
Audience: Grades K–6 and 7–12.
Focus: To reduce violence and promote caring and cooperative schools and communities through showing children that they have many choices for dealing with conflict other than through passivity or aggression, through teaching them skills to make real choices in their own lives, and through increasing their understanding and appreciation of their own culture and other cultures.
Key Teaching Strategies: Role-playing, interviews, group dialog, brainstorming, and other affective experiential learning strategies.
Type of Material: Curriculum, videos, resource material.
Cost: Curriculum not available for purchase without a 3- to 5-year commitment to the program within a school system. Videos are available from $24 to $40.

Appendix C: Conflict Resolution Reading List

Many of the publications listed in this appendix are available from the Office of Juvenile Justice and Delinquency Prevention's Juvenile Justice Clearinghouse, a component of the National Criminal Justice Reference Service (NCJRS). An NCJ (National Criminal Justice) number after a citation indicates that the publication is available from the Clearinghouse on microfiche or through paper reproduction or interlibrary loan. For further information, contact the Clearinghouse by telephone at 800–638–8736; via the electronic bulletin board at 301–738–8895; or through the Internet at askncjrs@ncjrs.org.

American Psychological Association. 1993. *Violence and Youth: Psychology's Response. Volume I: Summary Report on the American Psychological Association Commission on Violence and Youth.* Washington, DC: American Psychological Association. **NCJ 160391.**

Arbetman, L.P., E.T. McMahon, and E.L. O'Brien. 1994. *Street Law: A Course in Practical Law,* 5th edition. St. Paul, MN: West Publishing Company.

Banks, J. 1993. *Multi-Cultural Education: Issues and Perspectives,* 2d edition. Des Moines, IA: Longwood Division, Allyn & Bacon.

Banks, J. 1994. *Multi-Ethnic Education: Theory and Practice,* 3d edition. Des Moines, IA: Longwood Division, Allyn & Bacon.

Blechman, F. 1996. *Evaluating School Conflict Resolution Programs.* Fairfax, VA: Institute for Conflict Analysis and Resolution (ICAR), George Mason University.

Bodine, R., and D. Crawford. 1995 (March). "Our School's Choice: Creating Peace or Struggling with Violence." *Illinois Principals Association Building Leadership Practitioners Bulletin* 2:1–2, 5–6. **NCJ 160458.**

Bodine, R., and D. Crawford. In press. *Developing Emotional Intelligence Through Classroom Management: Creating Responsible Learners in Our Schools and Effective Citizens for Our World.* Champaign, IL: Research Press, Inc. **NCJ 160393.**

Bradley, S., and F. Henderson. 1994 (Spring). "A Calm Approach to Violence in the Schools." *Popular Government,* pp. 34–40.

Brekke-Miesner, P. 1994. *Keeping the Peace.* Oakland, CA: Oakland Unified School District, Office of Health and Safety Programs.

Brendtro, L., and N. Long. 1993 (Spring). "Violence Begets Violence: Breaking Conflict Cycles." *Journal of Emotional and Behavioral Problems,* pp. 2–7. **NCJ 160460.**

Brewer, D., J.D. Hawkins, R. Catalano, and H. Neckerman. 1994. *Preventing Serious, Violent and Chronic Juvenile Offending: A Review of Evaluations of Selected Strategies in Childhood, Adolescence and the Community.* Seattle, WA: Developmental Research & Programs. **NCJ 160394.**

Cahill, M. 1993. *Beacon School-Based Community Centers and Violence Prevention: A Discussion Paper.* New York, NY: Youth Development Institute. **NCJ 160396.**

Cardenas, J. 1995. *Multi-Cultural Education: A Generation of Advocacy.* Des Moines, IA: Longwood Division, Allyn & Bacon.

Cities in Schools, Inc. 1993. *Seeds of Hope: A Guide for Program Resources.* Alexandria, VA: Cities in Schools, Inc. **NCJ 160400.**

Community Board Program. 1992. *Starting a Conflict Managers Program.* San Francisco, CA: Community Board Program, Inc.

Crawford, D., R. Bodine, and R. Hoglund. 1993. *The School for Quality Learning.* Champaign, IL: Research Press, Inc. **NCJ 160406.**

Curwin, R., and A. Mendler. 1988. *Discipline with Dignity.* Alexandria, VA: Association for Supervision and Curriculum Development.

Davis, A. 1994 (Fall). *Justice Without Judges.* PC# 7380100 0803. Chicago, IL: American Bar Association, National Law-Related Resource Center.

Davis, A., and K. Porter. 1985 (Winter). *Tales of Schoolyard Mediation.* PC# 7380100 0901. Chicago, IL: American Bar Association, National Law-Related Resource Center.

Davis, A., and R. Salem. 1985 (Spring). *Resolving Disputes: The Choice is Ours.* PC# 7380100 0902. Chicago, IL: American Bar Association, National Law-Related Resource Center.

DeJong, W. 1994 (Spring). "School-Based Violence Prevention: From Peaceable School to the Peaceable Neighborhood." *Forum,* no. 25, pp. 8–14. **NCJ 149673.**

DeJong, W. 1994 (Fall). "Creating a More Peaceful World." *School Safety.* National School Safety Center (NSSC) News Journal. **NCJ 160463.**

Deutsch, M. 1973. *The Resolution of Conflict.* New Haven, CT: Yale University Press. **NCJ 160410.**

Diaz-Rico, L., and K. Weed. 1995. *The Crosscultural Language and Academic Development Handbook: A Complete K–12 Reference Guide.* Des Moines, IA: Longwood Division, Allyn & Bacon.

Dreyfuss, E. 1990 (Spring). *Learning Ethics in School-Based Mediation Programs.* PC# 7380100 1402. Chicago, IL: American Bar Association, National Law-Related Resource Center.

Fairfax County Public Schools. 1995. *Fairfax County Public Schools Task Force on Hispanic Youth and Gang Violence, Preliminary Report.* Fairfax, VA: Fairfax County Public Schools. **NCJ 160411.**

Fisher, R., W. Ury, and B. Patton. 1991. *Getting to Yes: Negotiation Agreement Without Giving In.* New York, NY: Penguin Books. **NCJ 160412.**

Frias, G. 1994. "Rhetoric and Realism: We Need a National Strategy for Safe Schools." *Harvard Education Newsletter* 3(3):4–5. **NCJ 160464.**

Gaustad, J. 1991 (October). "Schools Attack the Roots of Violence." *ERIC Digest,* no. 63. **NCJ 138814.**

Gaustad, J. 1992 (December). "School Discipline." *ERIC Digest,* no. 78. **NCJ 160466.**

General Accounting Office. 1995. *School Safety: Promising Initiatives for Addressing School Violence.* Washington, DC: U.S. General Accounting Office. **NCJ 160070.**

Girard, K., and S.J. Koch. 1996. *Conflict Resolution in the Schools: A Manual for Educators.* San Francisco, CA: Jossey-Bass, Inc., Publishers.

Glass, R. 1994 (February). "Keeping the Peace: Conflict Resolution Training Helps Counter Violence." *American Teacher* (a publication of American Federation of Teachers, AFL–CIO) 78(5):6–7, 15. **NCJ 160468.**

Grossnickle, D., and R. Stephens. 1992. *Developing Personal and Social Responsibility: A Guide to Community Action.* Malibu, CA: Pepperdine University Press. **NCJ 160415.**

Haberman, M., and V. Schreiber Dill. 1995. "Commitment to Violence Among Teenagers in Poverty." *Kappa Delta Pi Record* 31(4):148–156. **NCJ 160472.**

Hamburg, D. 1994. *Education for Conflict Resolution.* Report of the President. New York, NY: Carnegie Corporation of New York. **NCJ 154823.**

Hammond, R. 1994. *Dealing with Anger: A Violence Prevention Program for African American Youth.* Champaign, IL: Research Press, Inc.

Hawkins, J.D. 1992. *Social Development Strategy: Building Protective Factors in Your Community.* Seattle, WA: Developmental Research and Programs, Inc. **NCJ 160418.**

Hawkins, J.D., H.J. Doucek, and D.M. Lishner. 1988. "Changing Teaching Practices in Mainstream Classrooms to Improve Bonding and Behavior of Low Achievers." *American Research Journal* 25(1): 31–50. **NCJ 160474.**

Hechinger, F. 1994. "Saving Youth From Violence." *Carnegie Quarterly* 39(1):1–5. **NCJ 148902.**

Institute for Conflict Analysis and Resolution. 1994. *Understanding Intergroup Conflict in Schools: Strategies and Resources.* Fairfax, VA: Institute for Conflict Analysis and Resolution (ICAR), George Mason University. **NCJ 160420.**

Iowa Peace Institute. 1994. *Fostering Peace: A Comparison of Conflict Resolution Approaches for Students Grades K–12.* Grinnell, IA: Iowa Peace Institute.

Jenkins, J., and M. Smith. 1987. *School Mediation Evaluation Materials.* Albuquerque, NM: New Mexico Center for Dispute Resolution.

Johnson, D. 1994. *Cooperative Learning in the Classroom.* Alexandria, VA: Association for Supervision and Curriculum Development.

Johnson, D., and R. Johnson. 1993 (December/January). "Cooperative Learning and Conflict Resolution." *The Fourth R* 42:1, 4, and 8. **NCJ 160477.**

Johnson, D., and R. Johnson. 1995. *Reducing School Violence through Conflict Resolution.* Alexandria, VA: Association for Supervision and Curriculum Development. **NCJ 160421.**

Kirschenbaum, H. 1995. *100 Ways to Enhance Values and Morality in Schools and Youth Settings.* Des Moines, IA: Longwood Division, Allyn & Bacon.

Kohn, A. 1994 (December). "The Risks of Rewards." *ERIC Digest.* **NCJ 160478.**

Lantieri, L., and J. Patti. 1996. *Waging Peace in Our Schools.* Boston, MA: Beacon Press.

Leal, R. 1989. *The Next Generation of Campus Mediation Programs.* San Antonio, TX: Public Justice Department, St. Mary's University.

Leal, R. 1994 (November). "Conflicting Views of Discipline in San Antonio Schools." *Education and Urban Society* 27(1):35–44.

Levy, J. 1989. "Conflict Resolution in Elementary and Secondary Schools." *Mediation Quarterly* 7(1): 73–87. **NCJ 120961.**

Lockona, T. 1991. *Education for Character: How Our Schools Can Teach Respect and Responsibility.* New York, NY: Bantam Books.

Maxwell, J. 1989. "Mediation in the Schools: Self Regulation, Self Esteem and Self Discipline." *Mediation Quarterly* 7(2):149–155. **NCJ 123098.**

Miller, E. 1994. "Promising Practices: Peer Mediation Catches On, But Some Adults Don't." *Harvard Education Newsletter* 3(3):8. **NCJ 160483.**

Miller, S. 1993 (Winter). *Kids Learn About Justice by Mediating the Disputes of Other Kids.* PC# 7380100 1701. Chicago, IL: American Bar Association.

Moore, P., and D. Batiste. 1994 (Spring). "Preventing Youth Violence: Prejudice Elimination and Conflict Resolution Programs." *Forum,* no. 25, pp. 15–19. **NCJ 149674.**

National Association for Mediation in Education. *The Fourth R* (bimonthly newsletter published by the National Institute for Dispute Resolution, 1726 M Street NW., Suite 500, Washington, DC 20036).

National Institute for Dispute Resolution. 1994 (Spring). "Dispute Resolution, Youth and Violence" (special issue). *Forum,* no. 25. **NCJ 160439.**

National Institute of Justice. 1995 (March). *Research in Action: PAVNET Online User's Guide.* Washington, DC: U.S. Department of Justice, Office of Justice Programs, National Institute of Justice. **NCJ 152057.**

National School Safety Center. 1995. *School Safety Work Book. What Works: Promising Violence Prevention Programs.* Malibu, CA: National School Safety Center.

Oehlberg, B. 1995. "Cooperative Conflict Management Strengthening Families." *Resolution* 4:1. **NCJ 160485.**

Ohio Commission on Dispute Resolution and Conflict Management. 1994. *Conflict Management in Schools: Sowing Seeds for a Safer Society, Final Report of the School Conflict Management Demonstration Project 1990–1993.* Columbus, OH: Ohio Commission on Dispute Resolution and Conflict Management. **NCJ 149714.**

Pastorino, R. 1991. *The Mediation Process — Why it Works: A Model Developed by Students.* Grinnell, IA: Iowa Peace Institute. **NCJ 160444.**

Pettigrew, M. 1993. *Confronting Racial, Ethnic, and Gender Conflicts in the Schools.* Boulder, CO: University of Colorado, Conflict Resolution Consortium. **NCJ 160445.**

Pruitt, D. 1981. *Negotiation Behavior.* New York, NY: Academic Press. **NCJ 097338.**

Raffini, J. 1996. *150 Ways to Increase Intrinsic Motivation in the Classroom.* Des Moines, IA: Longwood Division, Allyn & Bacon.

Resolution (a journal published by the Ohio Commission on Dispute Resolution and Conflict Management, 77 South High Street, 24th Floor, Columbus, OH 43266).

Rogers, M. 1994. *A Series of Solutions and Strategies: Resolving Conflict Through Peer Mediation.* Clemson, SC: National Dropout Prevention. **NCJ 160447.**

Roush, D. 1996. "Social Skills Training in Juvenile Detention: A Rationale." *Juvenile and Family Court Journal* 49(1):1–20. **NCJ 160789.**

Schmidt, F., and A. Friedman. 1994. *Fighting Fair for Families.* Miami, FL: Peace Education Foundation. **NCJ 160448.**

Smith, M. 1991 (Spring). *Mediation and the Juvenile Justice Offender.* PC# 7380100 1502. Chicago, IL: American Bar Association, National Law-Related Resource Center.

Steele, P. 1991. *Youth Corrections Mediation Program, Final Report of Evaluation Activities.* Albuquerque, NM: New Mexico Center for Dispute Resolution. **NCJ 149709.**

Stephens, J.B. 1993 (Winter). "A Better Way to Resolve Disputes." *School Safety,* pp. 12–14. **NCJ 141656.**

Tennessee Education Association and Appalachia Education Laboratory. 1993. *Reducing School Violence: Schools Teaching Peace.* Charleston, WV: Appalachia Educational Laboratory. **NCJ 156514.**

Tolan, P., and N. Guerra. 1994. *What Works in Reducing Adolescent Violence: An Empirical Review of the Field.* Boulder, CO: University of Colorado, Institute for Behavioral Sciences. **NCJ 152910.**

Townley, A. 1994. "Introduction: Conflict Resolution, Diversity, and Social Justice." *Education and Urban Society* 27(1):5–10.

U.S. Department of Education and National School Boards Association. 1994. *Special Hearings on Violence in the Schools.* Proceedings of the National School Boards Association 54th Annual Conference and Exposition, New Orleans, LA. **NCJ 160452.**

Weitz, J.H., President's Committee on the Arts and the Humanities, and the National Assembly of Local Arts Agencies. 1996 (April). *Coming Up Taller: Arts and Humanities Programs for Children and Youth At Risk.* Washington, DC: President's Committee on the Arts and the Humanities.

Wilson, J.J., and J.C. Howell. 1993. *Comprehensive Strategy for Serious, Violent, and Chronic Juvenile Offenders.* Washington, DC: Office of Juvenile Justice and Delinquency Prevention. **NCJ 143453.**

Wilson-Brewer, R., S. Cohen, L. O'Donnell, and I. Goodman. 1991. *Violence Prevention for Young Adolescents: A Survey of the State of the Art.* Washington, DC: Carnegie Council on Adolescent Development, Carnegie Corporation of New York. **NCJ 160454.**

Wolfgang, C. 1995. *Solving Discipline Problems,* 3d edition. Des Moines, IA: Longwood Division, Allyn & Bacon.

Appendix D: Conflict Resolution Glossary

Active listening: A communication procedure wherein the listener uses nonverbal behavior, such as eye contact and gestures, as well as verbal behavior, including tone of voice, open-ended questions, restatements, and summaries, to demonstrate to the speaker that he or she is being heard.

Agenda: A list of items for discussion; issues or problem statements assembled in a sequence that facilitates efficient discussion and problem solving.

Aggression: Forceful action or attack.

Arbitration: Intervention into a dispute by an independent third party who is given authority to collect information, listen to both sides, and make a decision as to how the conflict should be settled.

Avoidance: The practice of nonengagement.

Basic needs: Needs that underlie all human behavior, such as survival, self-esteem, belonging, self-actualization, power, freedom, and fun. Like individuals, groups have basic needs, including the need for identity, security, vitality, and community.

BATNA: An acronym for Best Alternative To Negotiated Agreement, the standard against which any proposed agreement is measured.

Bias: A preconceived opinion or attitude about something or someone. A bias may be favorable or unfavorable.

Brainstorming: A storm of ideas. A group thinking technique for helping disputants create multiple options for consideration in solving a problem. Brainstorming separates the creative act from the critical one—all criticism and evaluation of ideas are postponed until later.

Caucus: A private meeting held with mediator(s) and disputant(s) to discuss needs and interests, the negotiating plan, and ways to make the procedure more productive.

Clarify: To make clearer or to enhance understanding. During a conflict resolution procedure, open-ended questions are often used for clarification.

Collaboration: Working with the other to seek solutions that completely satisfy both parties. This involves accepting both parties' concerns as valid and digging into an issue in an attempt to find innovative possibilities. It also means being open and exploratory.

Common interests/common ground: Needs and/or interests that are held jointly by the parties in a negotiation.

Community: A social group having common interests, identity, and customs.

Competition: A strategy in which one pursues the satisfaction of his/her own interests at the expense of others—a win-lose approach.

Compromise: Seeking an expedient settlement that only partially satisfies both people. Compromising does not dig into the underlying problem, but rather seeks a more superficial arrangement, e.g., "splitting the difference." It is based on partial concessions—giving up something to get something—and may have an underlying competitive attitude.

Conflict: An expressed struggle between at least two interdependent parties who perceive themselves as having incompatible goals, view resources as being scarce, and regard each other as interfering with the achievement of their own goals; a controversy or disagreement; coming into opposition with another individual or group.

Conflict resolution: A spectrum of processes that all utilize communication skills and creative thinking to develop voluntary solutions that are acceptable to those concerned in a dispute. Conflict resolution processes include negotiation (between two parties), mediation (involving a third-party process facilitator), and consensus decisionmaking (facilitated group problem solving).

Consensus: An agreement reached by identifying the interests of all concerned parties and then building an integrative solution that maximizes satisfaction of as many of the interests as possible; a synthesis and blending of solutions.

Consequence: A result that logically follows an action.

Cooperation: Associating for mutual benefit; working toward a common end or purpose.

Culture: That part of human interactions and experiences that determines how one feels, acts, and thinks. It is through one's culture that one establishes standards for judging right from wrong, for determining beauty and truth, and for judging oneself and others. Culture includes one's nationality, ethnicity, race, gender, sexual orientation, socioeconomic background, physical and mental ability, and age.

Deescalate: To engage in actions that decrease the intensity of a conflict.

Disputant: One who is engaged in a disagreement or conflict.

Diversity: The fact or quality of being distinct.

Empowerment: A method of balancing power in a relationship wherein the lower party acquires more power by gaining expertise, obtaining extra resources, building interpersonal linkages, and/or enhancing communication skills.

Escalate: To engage in actions that increase the intensity of a conflict.

Evaluation: The assessment of an option or possible conflict solution.

Facilitation: The use of a third party or parties to provide procedural assistance to a group attempting to reach consensus about a problem.

Framing: The manner in which a conflict solution or issue is conceptualized or defined.

Ground rule: A basic rule of behavior spelled out and agreed to at the beginning of a conflict resolution procedure.

Hidden interest: A basic need or want that is not immediately evident in a conflict situation, but that must be recognized and addressed before meaningful dialog can occur.

Integrative bargaining: The process of attempting to address and satisfy as many interests or needs as possible.

Interest: A substantive, procedural, or psychological need of a party in a conflict situation; the aspect of something that makes it significant.

Mediation: Intervention in a dispute by an impartial third party who can assist the disputants in negotiating an acceptable settlement.

Mediator: An invited intervener in a dispute whose expertise and experience in conflict resolution techniques and processes are used to assist disputants in creating a satisfactory solution. The mediator is a process guide whose presence is acceptable to both disputants and who has no decisionmaking power concerning the issues in the dispute.

Negotiation: An interaction between two or more parties who have an actual or perceived conflict of interest. In a negotiation, the participants join voluntarily in a dialog to educate each other about their needs and interests, to exchange information, and to create a solution that meets the needs of both parties.

Option: An alternative course of action; a possible solution that may satisfy the interests of a party to a dispute.

Peace: A process of responding to diversity and conflict with tolerance, imagination, and flexibility; fully exercising one's responsibilities to ensure that all fully enjoy human rights.

Position: A point of view; a specific solution that a party proposes to meet his/her interests or needs. A position is likely to be concrete and explicit, often involving a demand or threat and leaving little room for discussion. In conflict resolution, an essential activity is for participants to move beyond positions in order to understand underlying interests and needs.

Power: The ability to act or perform effectively.

Reframing: The process of changing how a person or party to a conflict conceptualizes his/her or another's attitudes, behaviors, issues, and interests, or how a situation is defined. Reframing during conflict resolution processes helps to mitigate defensiveness and deescalate tension.

Resolution: A course of action agreed upon to solve a problem.

Restraint: A method of balancing power in a relationship wherein the party with more power voluntarily refuses to use some of the power at his or her disposal.

Summarize: To restate in a brief, concise form. Summarizing is an aspect of active listening utilized by both disputants and mediators to increase common understanding.

Synergy: Cooperative thought and/or action of two or more people working together to achieve something neither could achieve alone.

Trust: To have confidence in or feel sure of; faith.

Value: A principle, standard, or quality considered worthwhile or desirable.

Violence: Psychological or physical force exerted for the purpose of injuring, damaging, or abusing people or property.

Sources: Schrumpf, F., D. Crawford, and R. Bodine. 1996. *Peer Mediation: Conflict Resolution in Schools,* revised edition, Champaign, IL: Research Press, Inc. Reprinted with permission from the authors and Research Press. Girard, K., and S.J. Koch. 1996. Appendix A. *Conflict Resolution in the Schools: A Manual for Educators,* pp. 135–139. Reprinted with permission from *Conflict Resolution in the Schools: A Manual for Educators,* K. Girard and S.J. Koch, copyright© 1996, Jossey-Bass Inc., Publishers, 800–956–7739.

Appendix E: Conflict Resolution in Schools Needs Assessment

Answer each question by providing the response that most accurately reflects your personal view of your school.

1. I am a: ❑ student   ❑ staff member   ❑ parent   ❑ other

2. Conflicts interfere with the teaching and learning process:

   ❑ often   ❑ sometimes   ❑ rarely

3. Problems between people at this school are caused by:

	often	sometimes	rarely
a. expectation to be competitive	❑	❑	❑
b. intolerance between adults and students	❑	❑	❑
c. intolerance between students	❑	❑	❑
d. poor communication	❑	❑	❑
e. anger and/or frustration	❑	❑	❑
f. rumors	❑	❑	❑
g. problems brought to school from somewhere else	❑	❑	❑

4. Without exceeding 100% as the total, estimate the percentage of problems referred for disciplinary action by the following categories:

a. between students	_____ %
b. between student and classroom teacher	_____ %
c. between student and other staff members	_____ %
d. between student and school rules	_____ %
e. other	_____ %

   Total   100%

5. Indicate the types and frequency of conflicts experienced by students in this school:

		often	sometimes	rarely
a.	put-downs/insults/teasing	❑	❑	❑
b.	threats	❑	❑	❑
c.	intolerance of differences	❑	❑	❑
d.	loss of property	❑	❑	❑
e.	access to groups	❑	❑	❑
f.	rumors	❑	❑	❑
g.	physical fighting	❑	❑	❑
h.	verbal fighting	❑	❑	❑
i.	school work	❑	❑	❑
j.	other: _____	❑	❑	❑

6. Indicate the effectiveness of each of the following actions in causing a student to change a problem behavior:

		very effective	somewhat effective	not effective
a.	time out	❑	❑	❑
b.	detention	❑	❑	❑
c.	conference with an adult	❑	❑	❑
d.	suspension	❑	❑	❑
e.	contacting parent(s)	❑	❑	❑
f.	expulsion	❑	❑	❑

7. Without exceeding 100% as the total, what percentage of influence do the following groups have in the way the school operates?

a.	students	_____ %
b.	teachers	_____ %
c.	parents	_____ %
d.	principals and school administrators	_____ %
e.	superintendents and district administrators	_____ %
f.	board of education	_____ %
g.	other	_____ %

Total   100%

8. In this school, I am generally:

	most of the time	about one-half of the time	not very often
a. treated fairly	❏	❏	❏
b. treated with respect	❏	❏	❏
c. given equal opportunity	❏	❏	❏
d. treated with compassion	❏	❏	❏
e. accepted	❏	❏	❏

9. I am allowed to solve problems that affect me:

❏ nearly always ❏ sometimes ❏ hardly ever

10. This school should do a better job teaching students to:

	definitely yes	maybe	definitely no
a. tell another person how you feel	❏	❏	❏
b. disagree without making the other person angry	❏	❏	❏
c. respect authority	❏	❏	❏
d. control anger	❏	❏	❏
e. ignore someone who is bothering you	❏	❏	❏
f. solve problems with other students	❏	❏	❏

11. When I need help, I ask for it:

❏ nearly always ❏ sometimes ❏ almost never

12. If I needed help, I think I could get it from:

	definitely yes	maybe	definitely no
a. a parent	❏	❏	❏
b. a brother or sister	❏	❏	❏
c. another family member	❏	❏	❏
d. a teacher	❏	❏	❏
e. a counselor	❏	❏	❏
f. another school staff member	❏	❏	❏
g. another adult	❏	❏	❏
h. another student	❏	❏	❏

13. I think this school has:

☐ more problems than most other schools
☐ about the same amount of problems as most other schools
☐ fewer problems than most other schools

Appendix F: Conflict Resolution Program/Curriculum Assessment Forms

General Information

Name of program: _____

Author(s): _____

Publisher's name, address, phone:

_____

_____

_____

Publication date: _____

Cost:

    Teacher material $ _____

    Student material $ _____

    Video material $ _____

    Other material $ _____

    Specify nature of other: _____

Target audience (check all that apply)

    Schools:

    ❏ Preschool students
    ❏ K–2d grade students
    ❏ 3d–5th grade students
    ❏ 6th–8th grade students
    ❏ 9th–12th grade students
    ❏ Parents
    ❏ Teachers
    ❏ Administrators
    ❏ Other school staff
    ❏ Other adults

Alternative schools:

❑ Students
❑ Staff
❑ Parents

Juvenile justice facilities:

❑ Youth
❑ Staff
❑ Parents

Instruction format:

❑ One-on-one
❑ Small group (<15)
❑ Classroom (15–30)
❑ Schoolwide

Other general descriptive information about curriculum/program:

Strengths and weaknesses:

Use the following forms to assess the curriculum/program in five critical dimensions.

Foundation Abilities of Conflict Resolution

The program provides for developing understanding of conflict and peace and for the development of orientation, perception, emotion, communication, and creative thinking and critical thinking abilities.

Degree to Which Skill/Concept Is Developed by the Program

Foundation Ability/Concept	Thoroughly	Well	Somewhat	Not at all	Comments
Understanding conflict	4	3	2	0	
Cooperation	4	3	2	0	
Appreciation for diversity and prejudice reduction	4	3	2	0	
Understanding peace	4	3	2	0	
Empathizing	4	3	2	0	
Dealing with perceptions	4	3	2	0	
Managing emotions	4	3	2	0	
Active listening	4	3	2	0	
Speaking to be understood	4	3	2	0	
Brainstorming	4	3	2	0	
Fairness	4	3	2	0	

Fundamental Principles of Conflict Resolution

The program incorporates and provides for the development of operational understanding of the four fundamental principles of conflict resolution.

Degree to Which Principle Is Incorporated Into the Program

Fundamental Principle	Extensively	Well	Somewhat	Not at all	Comments
Separate people from the problem.	4	3	2	0	
Focus on interests not positions.	4	3	2	0	
Invent options for mutual gain.	4	3	2	0	
Use objective criteria.	4	3	2	0	

Problem-Solving Processes of Conflict Resolution

The program provides training in and practice with the problem-solving strategies.

Problem-Solving Process	Major emphasis		Minor emphasis		No emphasis	
Negotiation	Yes	No	Yes	No	Yes	No
Mediation	Yes	No	Yes	No	Yes	No
Consensus decisionmaking	Yes	No	Yes	No	Yes	No

Learning Opportunities and Styles

Criteria for the learning process relate to the manner in which the curriculum is organized, delivered, and learned.

Learning Process Criteria	Degree to which criteria are satisfied					Comments
	Fully	To some extent			Not at all	
	100%	75%	50%	25%		
The program uses a variety of learning activities.	4	3	2	1	0	
The program offers opportunities to practice conflict resolution in day-to-day situations.	4	3	2	1	0	
Materials are age appropriate for the target population.	4	3	2	1	0	
Materials have clear formats and directions.	4	3	2	1	0	
Materials are culturally consistent for the target population.	4	3	2	1	0	
Materials are gender sensitive.	4	3	2	1	0	
Materials provide ideas for extending activities and learning beyond the materials.	4	3	2	1	0	
Materials offer opportunity or ideas for parental involvement.	4	3	2	1	0	
Materials contain ideas for integrating conflict resolution into standard school subjects.	4	3	2	1	0	

Implementation

Criteria for implementation relate to the efficacy of the information provided by the program to guide school personnel in the use of the materials and the program.

Implementation Criteria	Degree to which criteria are satisfied					Comments
	Fully	To some extent			Not at all	
	100%	75%	50%	25%		
Describes how to use the program.	4	3	2	1	0	
Describes appropriate audiences for the program.	4	3	2	1	0	
Describes how to address barriers to implementation.	4	3	2	1	0	
Offers startup ideas and suggestions for extending the program.	4	3	2	1	0	
Describes how to identify students for participation if only some students will be involved.	4	3	2	1	0	
Provides staff with suggestions for resources that offer additional information and strategies.	4	3	2	1	0	
Provides schedules and plans for training students.	4	3	2	1	0	
Provides practice activities in conflict resolution.	4	3	2	1	0	
Offers ideas for promoting the program within the school.	4	3	2	1	0	
Provides ideas for managing program operation.	4	3	2	1	0	
Delineates adult responsibilities in program operation.	4	3	2	1	0	
Provides ideas for obtaining sponsorships and financial support.	4	3	2	1	0	
Provides tools for assessing program effectiveness.	4	3	2	1	0	

Appendix G: Conflict Resolution Staff Development Provider Assessment Forms

Provider Assessment Form

General Information

Name of provider: _____

Organizational affiliation: _____

Provider address:

_____

_____

_____

Phone: (_____)_____

Fax: (_____)_____

Training based on specific published materials? ❑ Yes ❑ No

    If yes, title of materials: _____

    Authors: _____

    Publisher and publication date: _____

Materials included in training costs? ❑ Yes ❑ No

If no, cost:	Teacher materials:	$ _____			
	Student materials:	$ _____	Required?	❑ Yes	❑ No
	Video materials:	$ _____	Required?	❑ Yes	❑ No
	Other materials:	$ _____	Required?	❑ Yes	❑ No

Type of training provided:

Training audience:

Format of training:

Length of training:

Scheduling options:

Costs of staff development services:

Other general descriptive information about the staff development provider:

Strengths and weaknesses:

Provider Competency Assessment Form

Qualifications and training in conflict resolution:

Training in negotiation theory?   ❏ Yes   ❏ No

If yes, where received? _____

When? _____

Training in mediation?   ❏ Yes   ❏ No

If yes, where received? _____

When? _____

Experience:

Served as a mediator?   ❏ Yes   ❏ No

If yes, what were the experiences? _____

_____

School-based experience in education?   ❏ Yes   ❏ No

If yes, what were the experiences? _____

_____

Implemented a school conflict resolution program?   ❏ Yes   ❏ No

If yes, what types of programs? _____

_____

Number of years providing staff development in conflict resolution. _____

Has trained students in conflict resolution?	❏ Yes	❏ No
Has trained teachers in conflict resolution?	❏ Yes	❏ No
Has trained administrators in conflict resolution?	❏ Yes	❏ No
Has trained other school staff in conflict resolution?	❏ Yes	❏ No
Has trained parents in conflict resolution?	❏ Yes	❏ No

Approximate number of people that have been trained by staff developer: _____

Involvement in school reform initiatives?   ❏ Yes   ❏ No

If yes, what was the involvement? _____

_____

_____

Participated in the development of a strategic plan? ☐ Yes ☐ No

Facilitated the development of a strategic plan? ☐ Yes ☐ No

Has developed published materials? ☐ Yes ☐ No

Provides followup technical assistance and support? ☐ Yes ☐ No

    If yes, services? _____

    Costs? _____

Provide references for performance as staff development provider:

1) _____

_____

2) _____

_____

3) _____

_____

4) _____

_____

School representative may observe staff development provider conducting a training session prior to the school committing to a contract with the provider.

        ☐ Yes   ☐ No

    If yes, when? _____

    Where? _____

Appendix H: Strategic Planning Process

Schools and other organizations around the country are engaged in strategic planning on a regular basis. Such planning is valuable to the success of any endeavor and should be part of the implementation of any conflict resolution education program. The following information, which may be very familiar and second nature to many readers of this *Guide*, is provided to help readers who are not experienced in the strategic planning process to formulate a plan for bringing conflict resolution education into their setting.

Planning Process

A plan for a conflict resolution program is developed by the planning team in collaboration with the entire school faculty and is based on the results of the needs assessment. A planning team with broad-based school and community representation increases "ownership" of the program and commitment throughout the school community for its implementation. The planning process suggested here has four basic components: belief statements, a mission statement, program goals, and an action plan.

Belief Statements

Belief statements express fundamental convictions and tenets related to conflict and conflict resolution. They provide a basis for achieving consensus within the school community regarding a conflict resolution program in the school. The belief statements are the basis for obtaining the school's commitment to a specific mission to implement such a program. The following are sample belief statements:

- Conflict is a natural part of everyday life.

- Conflict is an opportunity to grow and learn.

- Neither avoidance nor violence are healthy responses to conflict.

- Through awareness of cultural differences, we grow to respect others and to cherish diversity.

- Adults provide powerful behavior models for students; this is especially true in dealing with conflict.

- Students can learn to resolve some of their conflicts without adult involvement.

Mission Statement

The mission statement is a broad declaration of the purpose of a conflict resolution program for the school. It is the cornerstone upon which the entire plan for the program is built. Often expressed as a single, brief, general statement, the mission statement articulates the primary focus of the program, emphasizes the distinctiveness of the program, and represents the commitment to the program. The following is an example of a mission statement:

> The mission of the conflict resolution education program is to teach students and faculty to resolve conflicts productively, to promote mutual understanding of individuals and groups throughout the school, and to enhance the climate of the school.

Program Goals: Adult and Student Outcomes

Goals are expressions of the desired outcomes of the conflict resolution program for students and adults in the school. The goals are the map for achieving the mission and give direction to all implementation planning. They guide the setting of priorities and provide the framework for evaluation of the program. The following are examples of program goals:

♦ Students will utilize the conflict resolution processes of negotiation, mediation, and consensus decision-making to resolve problems between students, between students and adults, and among groups.

♦ Adults will utilize the conflict resolution processes of negotiation, mediation, and consensus decision-making to resolve problems between students, between students and adults, between adults, and among groups.

Action Plan

The action plan delineates the tasks required to select and implement a conflict resolution program. It identifies the person responsible for each task, the timeline for completion, and the resources necessary. Development of the action plan is an ongoing process. As tasks are achieved, new tasks are delineated. The following is an example of an action plan format showing the initial steps in implementing a conflict resolution education program:

Task	Responsibility	Resources	Timeline
1. Preview program/ curriculum resource materials and select program(s)/curriculum(s).	Planning Team	Program/curriculum assessment forms. Budget: $200.	August–September
2. Interview and check references of staff development providers and select staff development provider/ trainer.	Planning Team	Staff development provider competency assessment forms. Budget: $20 (phone).	October
3. Train planning committee to develop program and use curriculum materials.	Planning Team Leader	Staff development budget. Budget: $2,500.	November
4. Provide faculty awareness in-service training on conflict resolution education.	Planning Team	Published materials, handouts, video rental. Budget: $300.	December

Appendix I: The Story of Little Red Riding Hood and the Wolf, Retold Through Negotiation

Step 1: Agree To Negotiate

RED: I'm Red Riding Hood. I agree to take turns talking and listening and to cooperate to solve the problem.

WOLF: I'm the Wolf. I agree to take turns talking and listening, and I agree to cooperate with you, Red Riding Hood, to solve the problem.

Step 2: Gather Points of View

RED: I was taking a loaf of fresh bread and some cakes to my granny's cottage on the other side of the woods. Granny wasn't well, so I thought I would pick some flowers for her along the way.

I was picking the flowers when you, Wolf, jumped out from behind a tree and started asking me a bunch of questions. You wanted to know what I was doing and where I was going, and you kept grinning that wicked grin and smacking your lips together. You were being so gross and rude. Then you ran away. I was frightened.

WOLF: You were taking some food to your grandmother on the other side of the woods, and I appeared from behind the tree and frightened you.

RED: Yes, that's what happened.

WOLF: Well look, Red, the forest is my home. I care about it and try to keep it clean. That day, I was cleaning up some garbage people had left behind when I heard footsteps. I leaped behind a tree and saw you coming down the trail carrying a basket of goodies.

I was suspicious because you were dressed in that strange red cape with your head covered up as if you didn't want anyone to know who you were. You started picking my flowers and stepping on my new little pine trees.

Naturally, I stopped to ask you what you were doing. You gave me this song and dance about going to your granny's house with a basket of goodies.

I wasn't very happy about the way you treated my home or me.

RED: You were concerned when you saw me in a red cape picking your flowers. You stopped me and asked me what I was doing.

WOLF: That's right.

RED: Well, the problem didn't stop there. When I got to my granny's house, you were disguised in my granny's nightgown. You tried to eat me with those big ugly teeth. I'd be dead today if it hadn't been for the woodsman who came in and saved me. You scared my granny. I found her hiding under the bed.

WOLF: You say I put on your granny's nightgown so you would think I was your granny, and that I tried to hurt you?

RED: I said you tried to eat me. I really thought you were going to eat me up. I was hysterical.

WOLF: Now wait a minute, Red. I know your granny. I thought we should teach you a lesson for prancing on my pine trees in that get-up and for picking my flowers. I let you go on your way in the woods, but I ran ahead to your granny's cottage.

When I saw Granny, I explained what happened, and she agreed that you needed to learn a lesson. Granny hid under the bed, and I dressed up in her nightgown.

When you came into the bedroom you saw me in the bed and said something nasty about my big ears. I've been told my ears are big before, so I tried to make the best of it by saying big ears help me hear you better.

Then you made an insulting crack about my bulging eyes. This one was really hard to blow off, because you sounded so nasty. Still, I make it a policy to turn the other cheek, so I told you my big eyes help me see you better.

Your next insult about my big teeth really got to me. You see, I'm quite sensitive about my teeth. I know that when you made fun of my teeth I should have had better control, but I leaped from the bed and growled that my teeth would help me to eat you.

But, come on, Red! Let's face it. Everyone knows no Wolf could ever eat a girl, but you started screaming and running around the house. I tried to catch you to calm you down.

All of a sudden the door came crashing open, and a big woodsman stood there with his ax. I knew I was in trouble . . . there was an open window behind me, so out I went.

I've been hiding ever since. There are terrible rumors going around the forest about me. Red, you called me the Big Bad Wolf. I'd like to say I've gotten over feeling bad, but the truth is I haven't lived happily ever after.

I don't understand why Granny never told you and the others my side of the story. I'm upset about the rumors and have been afraid to show my face in the forest. Why have you and Granny let the situation go on for this long? It just isn't fair. I'm miserable and lonely.

RED: You think that I have started unfair rumors about you, and you are miserable and lonely and don't understand why Granny didn't tell your side of the story.

Well, Granny has been sick—and she's been very tired lately. When I asked her how she came to be under the bed, she said she couldn't remember a thing that had happened. Come to think of it, she didn't seem too upset . . . just confused.

WOLF: So you think it is possible that Granny just doesn't remember because she is sick.

Step 3: Focus on Interests

RED: I want to be able to take flowers to Granny when I visit her because she is lonely and flowers help cheer her up.

I want to be able to go through the forest to Granny's house because it is too far to take the road around the forest.

I want you to stop trying to scare me or threaten me in the forest because I want to feel safe. Besides, I think the forest is a fun place.

WOLF: You want to go through the forest to visit Granny who is lonely, and you want to feel safe because you think the forest is a neat place.

RED: Yes, and I want to take flowers to Granny.

WOLF: I want you to watch where you are walking and to stop picking my flowers because I want to keep my forest home looking nice.

I want the rumors to stop because I want people to like me, and I want to be able to enjoy the forest without being afraid that someone is hunting for me.

RED: You want the forest to be pretty, you want people who visit the forest to like you and not be afraid of you, and you want to be safe in the forest.

WOLF: Right, the forest is my home. I should be free to enjoy my own home.

Step 4: Create Win-Win Options

RED: In order to solve this problem, I could try to stay on the path when I walk through the forest.

WOLF: I could try to remember to call out when I hear you coming instead of quietly stepping out from behind a tree. I could plant some flowers over by Granny's house for you to pick.

RED: I could pick up trash I see in the forest and take it to Granny's trash can.

WOLF: I could check up on Granny to make sure she is OK on those days when you can't make it. She is my friend, you see.

RED: Granny and I can talk to the woodsman and tell him we made a mistake about you. I could tell my friends that I'm not afraid of you anymore — that you can be nice.

WOLF: I could meet your friends on the edge of the forest and show them through it.

Step 5: Evaluate Options

WOLF: Do you think if you tell the woodsman and your friends that you made a mistake about me and that I'm really nice, then I won't have to worry about the woodsman and his hunters catching me?

RED: I think that will work.

WOLF: Maybe I could go with you to talk to the woodsman.

RED: Yes, that would help. You could also go with me when I tell my friends I'm not afraid of you anymore. . . . I'd like to help you plant some flowers at Granny's, and

I could also help you plant some in the forest. It would be nice to visit Granny together. She's pretty lonely.

WOLF: That sounds good.

RED: I agree.

WOLF: I don't think it will work for you to stay on the path all the time. I can show you where to walk so you don't harm anything.

RED: I think that's fair.

WOLF: I agree.

RED: Will it work for you to check on Granny when I can't visit her?

WOLF: Yes, if you call me early in the morning.

RED: I think it would be a good idea if I ask my friends for a donation when you give them a tour of the forest, and we could use the money to buy more trees to plant and start a recycling program for the trash we pick up.

WOLF: I think we've taken care of both of our interests.

RED: This solution will help both of us.

Step 6: Create an Agreement

RED: I'll arrange for Granny and myself to talk to the woodsman. I'll try to get an appointment for this afternoon, and I'll let you know when.

WOLF: I'll get some flowers to plant at Granny's. I'll have them ready to plant Saturday. I'll draw up a possible forest tour map and give it to you.

RED: As soon as I get your tour map, I'll bring some friends over to try it out. That's when I'll introduce you and tell them you're nice.

WOLF: I'll put a donations box at the edge of the forest for our tree planting and recycling program.

RED: And I'll call you by 7 o'clock if I can't go visit Granny.

WOLF: OK. I've agreed to get flowers to plant by Saturday, to draw a tour map of the forest, to go along with you to talk with the woodsman, to meet your friends and lead a tour through the forest, to take care of the donations box, and to visit Granny when you can't do it.

RED: I've agreed to arrange for an appointment with Granny and the woodsman, to plant flowers with you, to bring my friends to tour the forest and introduce you as a nice Wolf, and to call you by 7 o'clock if I can't visit Granny.

(The two shake hands.)

Source: Bodine, R., D. Crawford, and F. Schrumpf. 1994. *Creating the Peaceable School: A Comprehensive Program for Teaching Conflict Resolution.* Champaign, IL: Research Press, Inc., pp. 102–104, 106, 108, 110, 112. Reprinted with permission of the authors and Research Press, Inc.

Breinigsville, PA USA
02 March 2010
233483BV00001B/4/A